Suzuki at the TT Races

1960 to 1967

ELWYN ROBERTS with RAYMOND AINSCOE

Published in 2010 by Ilkley Racing Books
3 Mendip House Gardens Curly Hill Ilkley LS29 0DD

Suzuki at the TT Races: 1960 to 1967: ISBN 978-0-9524802-5-9

Printed by The Amadeus Press, Cleckheaton, West Yorkshire

Front cover: Frank Perris aboard Whispering Death, the square four 250 cc Suzuki, in the Lightweight TT, 1965. In accordance with our usual policy for front cover illustrations, Perris is pictured at Quarter Bridge. (FoTTofinders)

Back cover: Mitsuo Itoh and the factory's 50 cc RK67 of 1967 vintage, at Suzuki Sunday, 3rd June 2007, Castletown Golflinks Hotel, Fort Island.

About the authors:
A resident of Snowdonia, Elwyn Roberts has suffered a lifelong obsession (in its most severe form) with road racing. In his youth (a long time ago) he raced sidecars and subsequently he has sponsored many riders and contributed programmes and photographs to numerous articles and books. His collection of TT memorabilia featured prominently in Mick Duckworth's "TT100" and "The Island's Centenary TT exhibition" of 2007 in the Manx Museum in Douglas.

For almost thirty years, Raymond Ainscoe has contributed articles about classic racing to a variety of magazines (such as Legend Bike and Classic Racer). He is the author of "Gilera Road Racers" and "Laverda" for Osprey, as well as being a contributor to the Ilkley Racing Books series. He was the scriptwriter for the "Great Italian GP Racers" video. He parades and races classic bikes, usually a Gilera, over public roads circuits in the Netherlands and Belgium.

This book is number 400 of a limited edition of 500.

ACKNOWLEDGEMENTS

This book is to be launched at the 2010 TT, the fiftieth anniversary of Suzuki's debut in the Isle of Man TT races. It could not have been produced without the help of a number of enthusiasts, to all of whom we offer our thanks.

We must mention three Suzuki riders from the Golden Era, Frank Perris, Stuart Graham and Tommy Robb, all of whom kindly offered their hospitality and time to recall the heady days of the TT in the 1960s, when they were leading participants in the struggle for racing supremacy between the Japanese factories.

We are also very grateful to Ray Battersby, the author of the masterful "Team Suzuki", and his publisher Tim Parker, for their assistance in the publication of this book. And also to Mick Duckworth for his unprompted kind help.

The photographs have been culled from a variety of sources and we acknowledge the assistance of all copyright holders. (If, by mischance, we have failed to recognise a copyright, the holder is requested to contact the publisher.) A particular word of gratitude is owed to Frank Perris, not only for kindly writing the Foreword but also for the use of photos from his personal collection.

We also wish to thank former Manx GP rider and author Bill Snelling of FoTTofinders in Laxey and Walter Radcliffe of Ramsey (long-time TT marshal, sponsor and enthusiast) for the provision of shots from their archives. Do visit their photo exhibitions in Laxey and Ramsey held during TT and Manx GP fortnights. Other photos were kindly provided by Tony Breese of Racing Photos IOM.

Our thanks are also offered to Barbara and Stewart Clague of S.C.S. in Baldrine for their Manx hospitality and generous sponsorship of the Ilkley Racing Books series. Likewise to Mike Kelly and Alan Kelly of Mannin Collections Racing of Peel.

Elwyn Roberts and Raymond Ainscoe

FOREWORD

Having already had the chance to read the draft text of this book, I was delighted when I was approached by Elwyn and Raymond to provide a Foreword. My years with Suzuki were the most successful of my racing career and the TT was of course, in the 1960s, the highlight of each year's campaign. I feel that it is appropriate that this history of the Japanese factory's participation in the world's greatest road race is to be published to coincide with the marque's fiftieth anniversary of its debut in "Man Island" in 2010.

I count myself extremely fortunate to have played a part in Suzuki's first endeavours to claim Tourist Trophy and world championship honours and, as the team captain in those golden years, I was surrounded in the squad by highly talented team-mates, whom I count as my friends as well as former rivals. We certainly raced hard against each other, with no quarter asked or given, and against the teams from Honda, Yamaha and Kawasaki. But, when the racing was over, we would all be partying together in the evening, with the rivalries forgotten until the next meeting came along.

More than forty years have now passed since Suzuki Japan pulled out of the TT but my memories are still vivid, the friendships forged on the track and in the paddock have stood the test of time and of course Suzuki remains a major force to be reckoned with at the TT.

I hope that this book brings back recollections from that golden decade for those readers who were lucky enough to witness the titanic struggles for supremacy in the lightweight classes at the TT races in the 1960s; for the younger reader, I hope that it conveys a flavour of Suzuki's attempts to conquer the Mountain circuit and win a TT. For me, it rekindles many happy memories of a career in racing which took me all over the world, introduced me to many fascinating people and gave Rita and me wonderful lives, rich in experience.

Frank Perris
Suzuki team captain 1962-1966
Cwmparc, August 2009

Having concluded his works Suzuki career, Frank Perris rode the legendary four cylinder Gilera fire-engine in its final race appearance in the British Isles, the end of season 1966 Race of the South at Brands Hatch. His team-mate was the ex- Mondial, MV and Bianchi star Remo Venturi.

1960

In 1959, Honda ventured to the Isle of Man and, with their squad of Japanese riders, won the Manufacturers' Team Award for the 125 cc TT, held over the Clypse course. A couple of months later, the same riders and machines entered Japan's major competition: the Asama Plains Race, basically an endurance race over a mixture of volcanic ash roads and public highways. Honda, its machines duly shod with knobbly tyres, predictably dominated the 125 cc event, claiming the first four positions led home by Kitano. Languishing in a disappointing fifth place was Suzuki's sole survivor, Michio Ichino, on his Colleda RB.

But, from the ashes of that humiliating showing, Suzuki rose so that, merely ten months later, the marque also took its place on the starting grid of the world's foremost race, the Isle of Man Tourist Trophy.

Who were the key characters behind Suzuki's entry onto the world championship stage? First of all, President Shunzo Suzuki. He had instructed his engineers to enter Asama in the first place and indeed then authorised the establishment of a race shop and the design of a purpose-built racing motorcycle, overriding the objections of some of his colleagues on the Suzuki board who were not convinced that "racing would improve the breed" or that the costs of the exercise would be justified by the increased sales which might ensue.

Next, Takeharu Okana was to be a pivotal figure over the next few years. A former aircraft engineer and academic, Okana was recruited in 1958 specifically to prepare for the following year's Asama event. He was responsible for moving on from the policy of racing modified road bikes and designed the 125 cc two stroke single cylinder engine which was mated with a new twin down-tube chassis with swinging-arm rear suspension; the result was Suzuki's purpose-built Colleda RB - "Colleda" meaning "This is it" and "RB" for "race bike".

Another essential component was Akira "Jimmy" Matsumiya, a manager for Shell in Hamamatsu, who cajoled his masters into sponsoring the Asama races. Suzuki production machines were filled with Shell lubricants.

Surprisingly perhaps, some credit for Suzuki's appearance on the starting grids of the GPs must go to none other than Soichiro Honda who, seemingly impressed by the speed of the Colleda RB, in November 1960 suggested to President Suzuki that his team should race abroad.

So it was that at the turn of the year Shunzo Suzuki decreed that his team would compete in the TT races in 1960. Easier said than done. The first requirement was for funding, as Japan's exchange control restrictions threatened to jeopardise the exploit. Enter Jimmy Matsumiya, who was able to provide cash abroad via Shell Petroleum (Japan), together with the promise of free petrol and oil in the Isle of Man via Shell in London.

Also enlisted was the help of Shell-Mex BP's Lew Ellis, one of racing's noted trade barons, who provided yet more cash which would meet the team's running costs.

In February, Matsumiya and Yoshichika Maruyama (who had managed the company's fledgling race team in the mid 1950s) ventured to the Island on an exploratory visit, accompanied by Lew Ellis. They walked and drove around the Mountain circuit, filming and noting every corner. The idea of the cine filming was to give the riders as close an impression of the circuit a possible; accordingly, Matsumiya drove slowly with the camera running at half speed so that, once set at normal speed, the impression would be something close to racing pace. Indeed, Maruyama sat on the bonnet of the hired car so that he could bank the camera around the corners and thereby give an even more realistic impression. As it was snowing during the visit, Maruyama must have been determined.

The next personality on the scene was racing's greatest hero of the day: Geoff Duke. Matsumiya called on his services, to tell them where it would be damp under the trees even when the sun was shining, to suggest lines, to beware of bumps and so on.

Meanwhile, back in the factory, a new 125 cc racer was being built in haste. Designated the RT60, it featured an aircooled two-stroke (piston port), twin-cylinder engine (and Matsumiya had already been trying to get to the bottom of Walter Kaaden's technical secrets which had carried MZ to such speed in 1959), in a frame akin to that of the Colleda RB.

Matsumiya's advice resulted in changes to the design of the RT60 and his film, once edited to illustrate a continuous lap, was busy being studied by Suzuki's chosen trio of riders: Ichino, Mitsuo Itoh and Toshio Matsumoto. Meanwhile, the TT entry forms were completed; the box marked "manufacturer" was mistakenly completed with "Colleda" and the error was famously carried through to the TT programme (and even the august journal "The Motor Cycle").

Matsumiya was keen for the RT60 to be completed quickly because Geoff Duke was on his way to Hamamatsu. Invited by the Japanese Motorcycle Federation to demonstrate a 500 cc Manx Norton, Duke flew out in April to visit the Yamaha, Suzuki and Honda factories.

On Duke's arrival at Suzuki's HQ, he was instantly whisked to the Yonezu test track to try out one of the new models just tested by Ichino and Itoh. Nearly thirty years later, Duke wrote of his test ride "I was most impressed with the way the engine ran comfortably up to 11,000 rpm. It was exceptionally smooth throughout its range, and the surge of power from the engine once the 8,000 rpm mark was reached was most impressive. The gear change was both light in operation and very positive, while excellent brakes really retarded progress, and it was still possible to lock either wheel when a low speed was reached. I would say that, within the limits of road available, I had never ridden such a quick, conventional type of two-stroke."

Duly encouraged, the Suzuki team was ready for its first venture to "Man Island". At a distance of fifty years, the timetable of

Attired in borrowed (and too tight) leathers and helmet, Geoff Duke is pictured astride the 125 cc RT60 at the Yonezu test track, April 1960.

Duke surrounded by the Suzuki race hierarchy. Standing, third from the left is Masanao Shimizu, the designer of the RT60's engine; next to him is Itoh and then Takeharu Okano. To the immediate right of Duke is Matsumiya and next to him is Maruyama.

the squad's trip can be traced thanks to team member Hiroyuki Nakano who took a host of private photographs and kept a daily diary. (Staying loyal to Suzuki, by the mid-1970s Nakano had risen to be one of the company's leading engineering designers and he designed its first four-stroke bikes, the GS series.)

On 10th May, the three riders and their back-up team (including manager Okano and a squad of mechanics) flew from Haneda airport and, together with their RT60s, they arrived in Douglas on Friday 13th - one month before racing was due to begin.

Details of the RT60 had been described by "The Motor Cycle" of 24th March: "Inclined at angle of 30 degrees, each cylinder has a bore and stroke of 44 x 41 mm; compression ratio is 12 to 1, and bulbous reverse-cone megaphones are used. The quoted maximum speed is 94 mph. A six-speed gear box is built in unit with the engine. Frame and cycle parts are orthodox; the frame is of tubular duplex pattern with telescopic front and pivoted rear forks. The hubs are of full-width type. A neat dolphin fairing adds the finishing touch. Dry weight is said to be a mere 176 lb."

The race squad leaves Haneda airport.

Working within the bowels of the Fernleigh.

An interesting aside was that Honda (which entered both 125 cc and 250 cc races) and Suzuki agreed to work together as one unit for the TT. The proposal originated with the Midget Motors Manufacturers' Association of Japan, to encourage the industry generally. Supervising the four-stroke/two-stroke partnership of the rival concerns, in what was billed as the "Japanese Racing Team", was Shell's Jimmy Matsumiya.

Once in the Island, transported from London courtesy of Shell, Team Suzuki took up station at the Fernleigh Hotel in which they were joined, just before practice began, by another two-stroke squad: MZ, with its ace rider, Ernst Degner, who would soon come to play a crucial role in Suzuki's TT exploits.

Another Fernleigh Hotel resident was Tommy Robb, who recalled the Suzuki teamsters: "As well as meeting them in the hotel, my garage was near Suzuki's and they were lovely people. But there was one problem: they had brought all their food with them from Japan and they cooked it on a little stove which they lit up by their table in the dining room; the smell was bloody awful!" (They had probably heard tales of the Honda team members' dietary problems encountered in the Nursery Hotel in Onchan a year earlier. The Honda team manager Yoshitaka Iida explained the difficulty, "You can't go into battle on an empty stomach. Before we left, the Old Man told us "You're going as representatives of Japan, so don't embarrass us' and he made us study table manners. So we ate bad food with good manners. The meat was always mutton. We'd use hand gestures to ask the waitress what the meat was and the answer was inevitably 'Baa'.")

In the days before official practice began, the Suzuki newcomers would often each ride about six laps of the Mountain circuit on road bikes and, as early as 18th May, contact was made anew with Geoff Duke. Itoh explained, "He took us round the circuit explaining the racing lines, corner by corner, showing the braking points and when to use full throttle."

The first official practice session, on Saturday 4th June, was marred by Itoh's spill on the tram lines at the Bungalow. He woke up an hour later in Nobles Hospital with an injured right knee and facial abrasions.

A digression about names: after Mitsuo Itoh attended the Centenary TT, an article appeared in an august classic racing journal suggesting that his name is properly Mitsuo Ito but that his surname was printed in error as Itoh in the official 1960 TT programme and the error stuck for decades. The position is not that simple. Japanese script is not always easy to translate, and indeed the Japanese use sounds which are unknown to the English and vice versa. Itoh's surname is pronounced in Japanese with a long "o" (as in "abode"), not a short "o" (as in "job"). Hence, to express the long "o", the Japanese, when translating into English, may use a dash over the "o" or add the "h" or indeed write "Itoo". Similarly, Michio Ichino may appear as Itino Mitio (as the Japanese use the family name first and their "t" is sounded as a cross between the English "t" and "ch" sounds). As readers will no doubt be familiar with the use of Itoh, this script will abide by that traditional spelling.

Nakano-San, whose diary reveals the day by day exploits of the squad during its first venture into the GP arena.

But one mistake certainly did occur in the Isle of Man concerning Itoh's name. In much of the official literature for the 2007 TT (even including the programme for the Centenary Dinner at the Villa Marina), his forename had become Mitsui (sic) Itoh. (Mitsui is, in fact, known in racing motorcycle circles as a substantial Japanese company, occasionally associated with Yamaha.)

So, back to 1960. With Itoh stuck in hospital, alongside Degner and Eric Oliver who had also come to grief on the Mountain, the search was on for a replacement rider. Tommy Robb was sought out by Matsumiya, but he was contracted to Castrol and so ruled out of a ride on the Shell-sponsored Suzuki. In any event, he too fell at Windy Corner in practice, suffering a broken neck, and joined his Fernleigh co-resident in Nobles.

Meanwhile, the Liverpudlian TT regular Ray Fay was without a bike, as his expected 250 cc Bianchi had not arrived, and, approached by Lew Ellis, he jumped at the chance of a Suzuki ride - even if it was unpaid - and so became the first European to race a factory Suzuki.

It was not all hard work for the Suzuki boys; Nakano's diary records sightseeing visits to Peel castle and Castletown, and various games of softball with their opposite numbers in the Honda squad.

On Monday 13th June, Suzuki's TT race history began, somewhat inauspiciously, in the Ultra-Lightweight race, which was monopolised by the MV Agusta works squad, led home by the world champion, the peerless Carlo Ubbiali, at 86.10 mph. The works Hondas occupied the sixth to tenth berths. The Suzukis proved to be reliable if relatively slow, finishing Matsumoto in 15th (picking up the final bronze replica), Ichino in 16th and Fay in 18th.

A twist to the inaugural venture came when Itoh was advised by the medics that he was not fit to return with his colleagues to Hamamatsu. His solution? He escaped through a window at Nobles and, with garden shears, cut the plaster cast off his leg and hobbled back to the Fernleigh.

Forty seven years later, on his return to the Island for the Centenary TT, Itoh was reminded of his sojourn in Nobles when Tommy Robb presented him with a photograph of the pair of them in the Fernleigh's front garden, following their escape from Nobles; the Irish star understandably looked miserable - his head was encased in plaster. (See his entertaining autobiography "From TT to Tokyo", first published in 1974 and republished over a quarter of a century later when he was much in demand as a rider and a story teller in the burgeoning classic scene.)

The team left the Island on the Wednesday and, after a couple of days sightseeing in London, returned to Haneda airport.

The Suzuki and Honda friendly rivalry extended to games of softball.

Okano, Shimizu and the three riders relax in the Fernleigh's grounds.

Astride a road-going Colleda, the Japanese riders acquainted themselves with the Mountain circuit. Ramsey resident Walter Radcliffe snapped Itoh at the hairpin. (Walter Radcliffe collection)

The Colleda RT60.

The Suzuki team at the start of practice. Back row, left to right: Nakano, Shimizu, Matsumiya, Okano and Kamiya. Riders left to right: Matsumoto, Itoh and Ichino. (FoTTofinders)

The entry list from the Scorecard Booklet.

MONDAY, 13th JUNE.   **T.T. MOUNTAIN CIRCUIT.**

LIGHTWEIGHT (125) INTERNATIONAL—3 LAPS

113.2 Miles

The race will start at 10.00 a.m. and the competitors will be despatched in pairs at intervals as shown.

No.	Driver	Machine	Start Interval M. S.		1st Lap	2nd Lap	3rd Lap
1	G. Hocking (S. Rhodesia)	125 M.V. Agusta	00	00	....	....	....
2	S. M. B. Hailwood	125 Ducati	00	00	....	....	....
3	E. Degner (Germany)	123 M.Z.	00	10	....	....	....
4	L. Taveri (Switzerland)	125 M.V. Agusta	00	10	....	....	....
5	J. Hempleman (New Zealand)	123 M.Z.	00	20	....	....	....
6	*C. Ubbiali (Italy)	125 M.V. Agusta	00	20	....	....	....
7	B. Spaggiari (Italy)	125 M.V. Agusta	00	30	....	....	....
8	R. H. F. Anderson	125 M.V. Agusta	00	30	....	....	....
9	E. Crooks	123 M.Z.	00	40	....	....	....
10	A. Gandossi (Italy)	123 M.Z.	00	40	....	....	....
11	T. K. Kavanagh (Australia)	125 Ducati	00	50	....	....	....
12	G. Suzuki (Japan)	125 Honda	00	50	....	....	....
14	N. Taniguchi (Japan)	125 Honda	01	00	....	....	....
15	J. Redman (S. Rhodesia)	125 Ducati	01	10	....	....	....
16	T. H. Robb (Ireland)	125 Ducati	01	10	....	....	....
17		123 M.Z.	01	20	....	....	....
18	T. Tanaka (Japan)	125 Honda	01	20	....	....	....
19	T. Phillis (Australia)	125 Honda	01	30	....	....	....
20	M. Itoh (Japan)	125 Colleda	01	30	....	....	....
21	J. Grace (Spain)	125 Bultaco	01	40	....	....	....
22	S. Shimazaki (Japan)	125 Honda	01	40	....	....	....
23	F. Purslow	125 Ducati	01	50	....	....	....
24	T. Matsumoto (Japan)	125 Colleda	01	50	....	....	....
25	M. Ichino (Japan)	125 Colleda	02	00	....	....	....
26	M. Kitano (Japan)	125 Honda	02	00	....	....	....
27	A. Pagani (Italy)	125 M.V. Agusta	02	10	....	....	....
28	R. Thalhammer (Austria)	123 Rimi	02	10	....	....	....
29	J. Baughn	124 E.M.C.	02	20	....	....	....
30	P. J. Walsh	125 M.V. Agusta	02	20	....	....	....
31	K. Martin	125 Ducati	02	30	....	....	....
32	A. Wheeler	125 Ducati	02	30	....	....	....
33	R. Patrignani (Italy)	125 Ducati	02	40	....	....	....
34	R. A. Avery	124 Montesa	02	40	....	....	....
35	R. W. Porter	125 M.V. Agusta	02	50	....	....	....
36	R. J. G. Dickinson	125 Ducati	02	50	....	....	....
37	D. Whelan	125 M.V. Agusta	03	00	....	....	....
38	J. Gow	125 Ducati	03	00	....	....	....
39	K. Whorlow	125 M.V. Agusta	03	10	....	....	....
40	D. Holden	125 M.V. Agusta	03	10	....	....	....
41	J. A. Dugdale	125 Ducati	03	20	....	....	....
42	R. Moulton	124 Montesa	03	20	....	....	....
43	J. W. Dixon	125 Rumi	03	30	....	....	....

* Denotes previous Lightweight 125 c.c. T.T. winner.

Ray Fay aboard the injured Itoh's Colleda.

Michio Ichino

Having returned home, the members of the squad were greeted as conquering heroes; left to right: mechanic Yasunori Kamiya, Nakano, Itoh, Matsumoto, Ichino and Shimizu.

1961

For the next campaign, which was intended to embrace the entire GP series, Suzuki beefed up their efforts substantially. First of all, the management team was supplemented by the arrival of Mike Ishikawa, who was responsible for finance and travel, working with Masanao Shimizu, the head of the racing department, and Okana who was in overall charge.

1961 and Ichino on his 125 cc model, with Okano in supervisory mode. (FoTTofinders)

Matsumoto awaits 125 cc practice. (FoTTofinders)

Itoh and Masuda, 125 cc machines, feature in an evocative paddock shot. (FoTTofinders)

Second, Suzuki followed Honda's lead by recruiting western riders, accepting that the Japanese riders were inexperienced in the ways of top-flight road racing. South African star Paddy Driver was signed up for the beginning of the year to lead the Japanese riders and assist with the recruitment of top-notch aces.

Third, new bikes were available. Whereas 1960's machine had rear facing carburettors feeding piston controlled inlet ports, induction was now through rotary disc valves in the crankcases with the Mikuni-Amal carburettors mounted laterally in MZ fashion. Bore and stroke of the 125 cc RT61 model remained at 44 x 41 mm. Other features were a compression ratio of 12:1, magneto ignition with remote high-tension coils and a six speed gearbox. Bhp claims varied wildly, from 15 bhp at 10,000 rpm to 20 bhp at 12,000 rpm. Including the plastic fairing, which had large side bulges to clear the carburettors, weight was 172 lbs. Top speed was claimed to be 106 mph and tests at Hamamatsu led the squad to believe that the TT lap time could be reduced by three minutes.

The ultra-lightweight model was joined by the new RV61, its 250 cc sibling (56 x 50.5 mm; 28 bhp at 11,000 rpm, 198 lbs), which was similar in design, save that the exhausts were tapered on the larger machine.

Suzuki's entries (in 125 cc and 250 cc categories) for the 1961 series were Michio Ichino, Mitsuo Itoh, Shunkichi Masuda and Toshio Matsumoto, with three non-Japanese riders. Paddy Driver was to lead the team and he had recruited Alastair King. A seventh bike was entered but the jockey had not been confirmed by the end of May.

ALASTAIR KING

Born near Killearn, Stirlingshire, King will forever be associated with Bob McIntyre, with whom he ran for sponsor-engineer Joe Potts, operating out of a tiny workshop in Bellshill. Having entered a motor mechanic apprenticeship, he was called up by the Royal Marines and served overseas.

A rare shot of Alastair King aboard the 250 cc RV61. Is it Governor's Bridge?

King met McIntyre through membership of the Mercury MCC of Glasgow (- see the badges on their crash helmets -) and, when the latter signed for AMC for 1954, King picked up his private sponsor, Sam Cooper of Troon. King won that season's Clubman's Senior on a Gold Star and soon turned professional, racing bikes for Potts - which actually he usually maintained and tuned himself.

His year of grace was 1959, when, in the TT, he was second in the Senior race (held in torrential rain) and third in the Junior and won the one-off Formula One 350 cc event on a 7R.

His partnership with McIntyre flourished; the pair bought a filling station and garage in Ballat, Stirlingshire, while various specials were built in the Bellshill workshop. They tested their racing bikes on the one bit of public road in Scotland which was long enough to accommodate a 500 Manx on full bore: west from Bridge of Orchy in Argyllshire.

And, in 1961, works contracts came their way: both were signed up to ride the fast but overweight 350 cc Bianchi steeds: McIntyre was poached by Honda for its 250 cc campaign and Suzuki came after his mate.

But, when McIntyre died after his crash at Oulton Park in 1962, King called it a day. He demonstrated the McIntyre Matchless at the Memorial Meeting at Oulton Park a couple of months later and never raced again. He was killed in the mid-'70s in a car accident.

Almost inevitably given King's involvement, attempts were made by Suzuki to sign up his big buddy Bob McIntyre but the Flying Scot was committed to riding a 250 cc Honda for Reg Armstrong's satellite team and, despite a spin on the quarter litre Suzuki at Jurby airfield (- did Honda know? -), he was not over-keen on getting to grips with a temperamental two-stroke over the Mountain circuit.

But the seventh berth was filled when Lew Ellis introduced another Shell-sponsored rider to the team: the New Zealander Hugh Anderson, who was down to compete in the Senior and Junior races on Norton and AJS machinery. It was to prove to be an inspired choice.

The Japanese onslaught on the TT was gathering pace. The four stroke Hondas were now realistic contenders and the Yamaha marque was making its Manx debut in the two lightweight classes with its rapid two strokes. And the Motor Cycling Federation of Japan was represented on the TT jury by its vice president Kenzo Tada, who had ridden a Velocette to 15th place in the Junior race of 1930.

The 125 cc race kicked off the 1961 series on the morning of 12th June, and it was an unmitigated farce from Suzuki's point of view. Of the seven entries, four were non-starters, Itoh retired on the first lap and Masuda and Ichino followed suit on laps two and three respectively. Salt was rubbed into the wounds as Honda registered its first Tourist Trophy success, with the rival concern capturing the first five places, led home by Mike Hailwood, and the Yamahas proved to be reliable, with three finishers.

That afternoon, after the sidecar race won by BMW pair of Max Deubel and Emil Horner, Hailwood took his and Honda's second win in the 250 cc five lapper, but at least the Suzuki squad salvaged some pride. Matsumoto was a non-starter and Masuda, King and Driver all suffered first lap retirements. But, although Itoh's race was run by lap four, Anderson and Ichino came home in tenth and twelfth positions, collecting bronze replicas.

Paddy Driver aboard his RV61. And it is Quarter Bridge. (FoTTofinders)

Ichino plunges down Bray Hill on his 250. . . . (FoTTofinders)

. . . . and then rounds
Quarter Bridge.
(FoTTofinders)

Matsumoto, RV61 (FoTTofinders)

What had gone wrong? To quote the doyen of racer-journalists Vic Willoughby, "No engines suffer worse from the narrowness of the power band than do the Suzukis. For instance, the two-fifty gives its best power at 9,500 to 10,000 rpm but is virtually useless below 8,500 rpm. Hence the clutch has a hard time on slow corners and the six speeds are anything but a luxury. For all that, acceleration is startling and top speed close on 120 mph though both fall off when misfiring sets in once the engine gets hot. Since the misfiring sometimes responds partially to half closure of the throttle, it may have its origin in carburation or the inability of the ignition to cope with maximum cylinder pressure."

Willoughby concluded that "the Nipponese. . . . seem to be still groping in the dark gloom of two stroke mysteries."

The Suzuki team was at a crossroads when it was approached by the two-stroke guru, Dr Joe Ehrlich. Dr Joe's EMC machines were fast (as Mike Hailwood and Paddy Driver were to prove) but Suzuki was not satisfied that he could cure the reliability problems and so rejected his advances. But a saviour was at hand: Ernst Degner.

ERNST DEGNER

Matsumiya shared an interest in jazz with his Fernleigh co-resident, Ernst Degner who, aboard Kaaden's MZ, was challenging for the 125 cc world title. In the few spare minutes when his Communist Party minders let him off the leash, Degner explored the possibility of defecting. In a meeting at the Castle Mona hotel, company president Shunzo Suzuki and Okano gave Matsumiya the go-ahead to recruit the East German.

Of course, a couple of months later, with his family smuggled into West Germany in a car boot, Degner fled from the Swedish GP paddock and joined them in Saarbrucken. He obtained a West German passport - and did not defect to Japan as has often been written.

With Degner, Suzuki acquired not only a top-flight rider but, more importantly, all MZ's secrets. There were reports that Degner presented Suzuki with drawings and an MZ piston and cylinder, although he subsequently denied that he had broken his contract in such a manner.

Degner's betrayal of Walter Kaaden came at a cost. He was still in line to win the ultra-lightweight world title, needing to beat Phillis in the final round in Argentina. But his plans went awry. Joe Ehrlich agreed to provide an EMC, but it was held up in New York airport customs. Frustrated in Buenos Aires, in any event Degner could not ride as the East German Federation suspended his licence and the organisers would not recognise his West German licence. So Phillis rode to his title - only for the embarrassed organisers to present him with his championship trophy inscribed "Tom Phillips".

Degner's career was truncated by a practice crash in the Japanese GP of 1963 which required 56 skin grafts and left him permanently scarred. He was obliged to miss the 1964 season and was never again a serious contender. He moved to the Canary Islands and set up a business renting Suzuki jeeps to tourists. But his wife left him and he became increasingly reclusive. He committed suicide in the mid-1980s - although the conspiracy theorists suspected KBG involvement in his passing.

Sadly, one man never forgave him. His patron, Walter Kaaden, regarded as the father of the racing two-stroke, felt deeply betrayed by the defection, saying "What disturbs me is that Degner took the results of our work, our love, and sold it. It wasn't his to sell."

1962

With Degner's involvement, three new models were prepared for 1962. For the inaugural 50 cc world championship series, Suzuki's offering was the RM62, an air-cooled inclined single cylinder rotary valve two stroke, with 40 x 39.5 mm bore and stroke. Features included an eight speed gearbox, a Mikuni carburettor, 8 bhp at 10,500 rpm, weight of 32 lb. And top speed of 83 mph.

The 125 cc bike, the RT62, was in essence an enlarged version of the tiddler, with 54 x 54 mm for the single cylinder, with seven speeds, 20 bhp at 10,500 rpm, top speed of 106 mph and 165 lb. in weight. Two engine types were built; the standard front exhaust version and a rear exhaust version, plagiarised from MZ and which Degner claimed offered better acceleration.

The parallel twin cylinder 250 cc RV62 was a doubled up 125, featuring six speeds, 42 bhp, top speed of 131 mph and 237 lbs. All three bikes employed a conventional duplex tubular cradle frame.

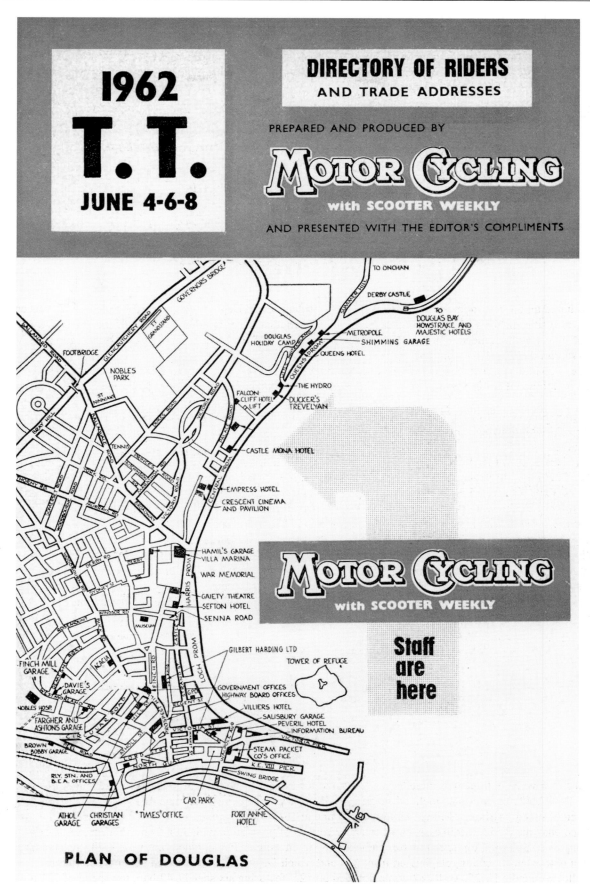

In the "good old days", "Motor Cycling" published a list of the riders' hotels.

FRANK PERRIS

Born to English parents in Toronto on 28th May 1931, Frank Perris passed his infancy in the USA and Canada but Chester was the scene of the majority of his childhood, as his father returned to the UK in search of work.

His first race was at a local circuit, Rhydymwyn, at a meeting which was notable as it saw the debut of a number of talented racers such as Steve Murray, Ralph Rensen and Terry Shepherd.

1952 was a key year for the youthful Perris: an international debut at Tubbergen aboard a pre-War KTT Velocette (ridden there from home in London and back) and a debut over the Mountain circuit in the Clubman's TT on a Triumph. He was signed by Jock West to ride a works AJS in the Ulster GP of 1955 and enjoyed a contract for 1956.

In 1959, he joined the Continental Circus, travelling with his German-born wife Rita across Europe in their van, with 350 cc and 500 cc Manx Nortons tuned by Ray Petty, living in an old army tent. He recalled, "The only rider who had a caravan in those days was Dickie Dale, who was very up-market living in such luxury."

Riding in world title races in 1961, Perris finished the season in third place (behind MV's Hocking and Hailwood) in the premier 500 cc class. He pestered Matsumiya for a Suzuki ride, initially without success, but when Hugh Anderson was injured Perris was recruited for the Belgian GP. "I was fifth in practice on the 250. I managed to be quicker than Paddy Driver, because I discovered that the top speed was achieved with the throttle rolled back a little bit. Paddy asked me how I managed to be so fast but of course I wouldn't tell him."

Perris secured a contract for 1962 but, notwithstanding Degner's skills, the bikes were still far from perfected. "The French GP was held at Clermont Ferrand, which was an extremely dangerous circuit, surrounded by cliffs and drops. The 125 cc and 250 cc bikes both seized in practice, throwing me off. Then, during the 125 race, held in atrocious conditions, I was pitched off again and slid up the road at about 200 kph. I have no idea how I survived; I had no injury but was covered in mud. As I walked back to the pits, I met Joe Ehrlich who had been watching Rex Avery on the EMC; he offered me a swig from his bottle of whisky, and of course I started drinking."

"When I got back to the pits, the first person to greet me was Okana; we did not get on too well - possibly because he had suffered a British bullet in his lung and he still bore a grudge. Anyway, he asked me how the bike was. I was furious - and a touch sozzled by then. His wretched bikes had thrown me up the rode three times and nearly killed me. I threw my helmet at him and stormed off."

Despite these inauspicious beginnings, Perris became the team's official captain until his contract ran out at the end of the 1966 season. Thereafter Perris rode the outdated Gilera four in its swansong at Brands Hatch in 1966, established a successful building company (Perwood) in South Africa in partnership with Mike Hailwood, came back to the TT to ride Suzukis for Eddie Crooks, managed the John Player Norton squad and then embarked on a variety of business ventures. Frank and Rita Perris retired to live in South Wales and in recent years he has been an active participant in classic parades.

Anderson passes through Ramsey, 1962, 125 cc TT.

To Ernst Degner, seen here on his "tiddler" pulling out of Governor's Bridge, fell the honour of recording Suzuki's first TT victory.

Seichi Suzuki plunges down Bray Hill on his way to eighth place in the first ever 50 cc world title event. (Walter Radcliffe collection)

14   *" Examiner " T.T. Special, Friday, 8th June, 1962.*

E. DEGNER WINS THE FIRST 50c.c. T.T.

FASTEST LAP at 75.52 m.p.h.

By G. S. DAVISON

ERNST DEGNER gave Germany victory on a Japanese Suzuki in the first 50 c.c. T.T. today at an average speed of 75.12 m.p.h. for the two laps, his fastest being 75.52 m.p.h.

He led all the way, with Swiss Luigi Taveri and Irishman Tommy Robb on Hondas taking second and third places.

ERNST DEGNER, winner of the 50 c.c. T.T. in action on his Suzuki today.

The Press Box, Friday.

At 11 o'clock the first ever 50 c.c. T.T. race is due to start, and it will be watched by many thousands of very interested spectators.

There has been much discussion about this event, and many differences of opinion. Some say it is ridiculous. Some say it is a magnificent stimulant to the the T.T. races; some don't like women being allowed to compete, some wish there were more of them. And so on.

No one can say that the race will be a flop when it has so many entries, some of which will be taking corners at well over the 80 mark and coming down the Mountain in the 90's.

As a matter of interest the entries are composed of 14 different makes. Itoms head the list with 15, Hondas and Kreidlers have nine each, and Derbis and Suzukis four each. Three-a-piece are contributed by Benellis, Fruin-Dartelas and Tomos, two by DOTs and one each by "BITS" Chisholm-Itom, Ducson, M.Z. and Tohatsu.

Unfortunately several machines could not be got ready in time, so that the Tomos and Derbis, amongst others, are non-starters. All the non-starters—24 of them are shown in the list of entries on this page.

So the field is down to 33, but this is enough to provide a most exciting race.

Best performances in Practice were as follows:—

E. Degner (Suzuki)	30 42.6	(73.72 m.p.h.)
L. Taveri (Honda)	31 20.2	(72.26 m.p.h.)
M. Itoh (Suzuki)	31 35.2	(71.69 m.p.h.)
M. Ichino (Suzuki)	31 54 8	(70.95 m.p.h.)
K. Takahashi (Honda)	32 13.6	(70.27 m.p.h.)
T. Robb (Honda)	32 33	(69.57 m.p.h.)

On their very first Practice period on Tuesday last week we timed the "Wasps" on the Sulby Mile. Taveri was fastest at 86.97 m.p.h., whilst Degner and Itoh clocked 85.71

The next evening we timed them up the 8-mile Mountain climb from Ramsey to Brandywell Corner, when here Taveri was again fastest, with a speed of 66.66 m.p.h. against Degner's 64.76.

The much publicised woman rider Mrs Beryl Swain, was only out on the first two occasions for she was unwell for the third and final period last Saturday morning. She was therefore unable to do more than three laps, the best of which was 47 mins. 23.6 secs., at a speed of 41.77 m.p.h. Over the Sulby Straight we clocked her at

54.22 m.p.h. and up the Mountain climb at 44.12.

Latest hospital reports—Takahashi is progressing favourably, but Thalhammer, who was involved in a road accident early last Monday morning, and Eccles who crashed on the second lap of Wednesday's Junior are born critically ill.

10.30 a.m. — The warm-up maroon — and the Wasps begin to sting; the whole nest sounds somewhat angry !

There are two Manufacturers' Teams — Kreidler with Anscheidt, Shorey and Huberts, and Suzuki with Degner, Ichino and Itoh. Curiously enough there is no Honda team. There are three Club Teams — Bemsee, Racing "50" M.C.C. and Wirral "100" M.C.

10.55 a.m. — the Five Minute maroon, and the the usual form, three, two, one—"good luck to you all", but no mention of 'may the best man win'—possibly because there's a woman in it !

The flags up, and Degner screams away. Derek Minter gets off alongside M. Ichino, and has a 20 yard lead over the Jap on the approach to St. Ninian's.

These 12 speed Kreidlers seem to change gear every few yards—which they'll obviously have to do if they want to get into top by Bray Hill !

All get away well until No. 42, S. G. W. Lawley, whose Itom is reluctant to start. He gets going finally just as the last man, W. D. Ivy pushes off; but Ivy's machine is also a slow starter, so he remains "last on the roads."

11.5 a.m.—The Steam Packet Co. announces that record numbers of vehicles have arrived for this year's T.T. — 1,002 cars, as against 734 last year, and 5,063 motor-cycles compared with 4,465 in 1961. It's certainly a motorcyclist's week!

Ernst Degner (No. 2) is first at Sulby Bridge. His team-mate Ichino is here next, 24 seconds later, so has lost 14 seconds in the first 20 miles. Anscheidt (No. 6) follows Ichino, and then comes Tommy Robb (No. 8) and Luigi Taveri (No. 10). Derek Minter (No. 3) who started 10 seconds behind Degner reaches Sulby 70 seconds after him ,so has lost a full minute.

The first retirements — H. L. Fruin and S. G. W. Lawley (who was a slow starter); both of them pack up at Quarter Bridge with engine trouble, both O.K., of course.

At 11.25 a.m. (approx.) Degner reaches the Bungalow, some forty seconds ahead of Ichino—i.e., half a minute on corrected time. Anscheidt (6), Robb (8) and Taveri (10) come past a few seconds later, all fairly close together; Robb and Taveri are certainly going some !

11.29 a.m. (approx.)—Degner is at Signpost, and just over a minute later he screams past the pits, having lapped in approximately 30 minutes. Wait for his lap time.

Ichino is next along some 40 seconds behind Degner, and then comes Tommy Robb, only about three seconds after Ichino. Degner is obviously leading the race, with Taveri second and Tommy Robb third.

Degner's lap time was 30 mins. 17.8 secs., at a speed of 74.72 m.p.h.—quite a bit better than the fastest lap in Practice. Tommy Robb is 15.6 seconds behind Ernst, but Taveri is only 15.2 seconds back· A close thing for second place ...

Three Suzukis, two Hondas and a Kreidler in the first six. Seventh is W. Gedlich (Kreidler), 8th J. T. Huberts (Kreidler), 9th S. Suzuki (Suzuki), 10, S. Shimazaki (Honda), 11th D. W. Minter (Honda) and 12th, D. F. Shorey (Kreidler).

1ST LAP LEADERS

		m. s.
1. E. Degner (Suzuki)		30 17.8
	(74.72 m.p.h.)	
2. L. Taveri (Honda)		30 33.0
	(74.10 m.p.h.)	
3. T. Robb (Honda)		30 33.4
	(74.09 m.p.h.)	
4. H. G. Anscheidt (K'ler)		30 45.2
	(73.60 m.p.h.)	
5. M. Inchino (Suzuki)		30 50.6
	(73. 39 m.p.h.)	
6. M. Itoh (Suzuki)		31 06.6
	(72.77 m.p.h.)	

It seems that Beryl Swain is not going too well, for she is still shown at Ramsey whereas No. 57, P. R. Horsham who started 20 seconds after her has passed the Bungalow.

11-44 a.m. — Here's Beryl at the Bungalow. So she's still going O.K.

At 11.50, Beryl is shown at Signpost, and here she is past the pits, having overtaken seven

"male drivers" on the first lap. Her lap time is announced as 46 mins. 57.4 secs., at 48.21 m.p.h.

By 11.52, the first half dozen on the roads have passed Ramsey and are climbing the Mountain for the second — and last — time.

Two more retirements — P. R. Horsham at the Creg and M. C. T. Sampson at Ramsey; both on Itoms and both O.K. So far there have been only four retirements, but a few riders may still be on their first lap, and may well be marked "R" before long.

11.59 p.m. (approx.) — Degner is at Signpost and now at 12 noon almost spot on, he comes past to win the first- ever 50 c.c. Tourist Trophy race.

One more retirement—the last man in the race, W. D. Ivy, at Creg Willy's with engine trouble, rider O.K., of course.

Next to finish are Taveri (No. 10) Anscheidt (No. 6) and Robb (No. 8)—close together and in that order. Taveri is obviously second, Robb third and Anscheidt fourth.

Degner's second lap is a new record at 75.52 m.p.h., and in under the half-hour — 29 mins. 58.6 secs., and his average for the race is 75.12 m.p.h. This speed would have won him a Bronze Replica in the Lightweight (125) race.

The first three come up on the raised platform, and Degner is garlanded. He says a few words." in very good English, too.

Meanwhile a dozen or more riders are still around the course, and one of them A. J. Pink (Itom) has retired at Glentrammon with engine trouble, rider O.K.

RESULT

		h. m. s.
1 E. Degner (Suzuki)		1 00 16.4
	(75.12 m.p.h.)	
2. L. Taveri (Honda)		1 00 34.4
	(74.75 m.p.h.)	
3. T. Robb (Honda)		1 00 47.6
	75.48 m.p.h.	
4. H. G. Anscheidt (Kreidler)		1 00 55.4
	(74.32 m.p.h.)	
5. M. Itoh (Suzuki)		1 02 00.4
	(73.02 m.p.h.)	
6. M. Ichino (Suzuki)		1 02 01.4
	(73.00 m.p.h.)	
7. J. T. Hurberts		1 02 15.6
	(Kre'dler)	(72.70 m.p.h.)
8. S. Suzuki (Suzuki)		1 02 31.8
	(72.38 m.p.h.)	
9. D. Minter (Honda)		1 04 06
	(70.61 m.p.h.)	
10 S. Shimazaki		1 04 15.2
	(Honda)	70.45 m.p.h.
11. D. F. Shorey		1 04 49
	(Kreidler)	(69.83 m.p.h.)
12. W. Gedlich		1 10 50
	(Kreidler)	(63.90 m.p.h.)
13. M. J. Simmonds		1 14 48.8
	(Tohatso)	(60.50 m.p.h.)
14. H. Crowder		1 15 29.6
	(Kreidler)	(59.96 m.p.h.)
15. R. Bryans		1 16 52.6
	(Benelli)	(58.90 m.p.h.)
16. C. W. W. Mates		1 17 10.6
	(Itom)	(58.65 m.p.h.)
17. G. B. Brader		1 25 34.2
	(Itom)	(52.60 m.p.h.)
18. P. R. Latham		1 26 04.6
	(Itom)	(51.91 m.p.h.)
19. H. Cosgrove		1 27 50.4
	(Itom)	(51.55 m.p.h.)
20. D. A. Juler		1 30 00.6
	(Itom)	(50.31 m.p.h.)
21. J. D. Lawley		1 32 53.4
	(Itom)	(48.75 m.p.h.)
22. Mrs B. J. Swain		1 33 41.4
	(Itom)	(48.33 m.p.h.)
23. P. Hardcastle		1 33 48.0
	(Itom)	(48.27 m.p.h.)
24. J. W. Waller		1 38 36.2
	(Itom)	(45.92 m.p.h.)
25. R. H. Bacon		1 49 49.4
	(Bits)	(41.23 m.p.h.)

Record Lap: Degner's second, in 29 mins. 58.6 secs., at 75.52 m.p.h.

Manufacturers' Team Prize: Suzuki (Degner, Ichino and Itoh).

No Club Team Prize was awarded.

TECHNICALITIES OF THE "FIFTIES"

by Peter Arnold (of "Motor Cycle News").

Greatest interest prior to the start of practice was centred around the Kreidler machines, following their successes in the Spanish and French G.P.'s, With their complicated and mysterious 12-speed drive, it was felt that they would be best served on the Mountain climb, which was acknowledged by the pundits as being the place where the race would be won or lost.

In their camp at the Derbyhaven Hotel, the Kreidler team of mechanics and technicians went to great lengths to ensure that no photographs were taken of the racing engine units, or of any part stripped from the many machines in the outside workshop. Nor would they commit themselves, when asked to explain how the gearbox worked. What goes on inside the 'box' is still very much a guarded secret. What is known is how the thing works—in theory !

A four-speed gearbox has an overdrive assembly fitted in unison with it, through which three variations can be 'played'. Bottom gear in the gearbox can thus be improved three times before a change into second is effected. The normal foot-change mechanism is fitted on the left for all riders except Dan Shorey, whose machine has a right-hand conversion. The over-driving is done via a handlebar cable operated control, similar to the scooter and moped idea, with the clutch lever and selector revolving around the handlebar. The two-stroke engine is fed through two carburetters, the twist

grip control having a separate cable to each. Like so many of the other 50's, 19 inch wheels are fitted back and front, with the minimum 2 inch section.

Interesting is the variable damping available on the front and rear suspension units, which can be fitted into any one of six positions on the serrated spring cover. The method of 'hanging' the engine and gearbox unit in the full loop duplex frame is worthy of note, as is the 'smoked' perspex screen. Each machine carries a spare plug fitted in the plug spanner and carried on the fairing mounting bracket above the steering headstock.

The Japanese Suzuki machine caused something of a surprise when they headed the practices leader board, the two-stroke engines obviously having improved output since the Ernst Degner regime, and it was he who lapped at 73.72 m.p.h. These machines are fitted with six-speed gearboxes.

The Hondas have been the object of many modifications since their defeats in the two Continental G.P.'s; in just over three weeks an 8-speed gearbox has been developed; the bore and stroke of these four-valve, double-knocker four-stroke engines has been varied to produce over 13,500 r.p.m.!

One of the most interesting machines in the race is the R. H. Bacon's "Bits". The standard Itom engine/gearbox unit is fitted into

a 1951 B.S.A. Bantam duplex rigid frame with Webb patern girdertype front forks. The gearbox has been converted to 4-speed, and the three gallon tank is an ex-E.M.C.-Puch. This unfaired machine cost its owner lessthan £30 — and it "cleaned up" at a recent Snetterton 50 c.c. meeting!

A man with a sense of humour is Harry Crowder, who has named his Kreidler Moped engined machine the "Shuttleworth Special"— shades of George Formby in " No Limit" ! This home-brewed job has a huge, square-shaped tank fitted and looks rather ungainly.

The Dot-produced Verbeti-engine machine is one of the first British manufacturers' attempts to crash into the 50 c.c. range, and is neatly prepared. The engine breathes through an Amal .G P carb., fitted with a ⅜-in choke.

Two-strokes dominate the class, only the Hondas being four-strokes. Most machines use either 18-in. or 19-in. wheels, and most—because they are Itom based—are three speeders, with the normal handlebar change. One that has six speeds is the Fruin-Dartela, which has a two-speed Albion box acting as a countershaft to the three-speed Demm engine-gearbox unit.

The wasps are new to the Island; so are most of the competitors. But if the race lives up to the practice promise, they'll be back, and the experience gained will produce even more interesting machines next year. Racing does improve the breed.

ENTRIES IN THE 50 c.c. RACE

1.	Honda (NS)		31.	C. C. W. MATES	Itom
2.	E. DEGNER	Suzuki	32.	J. W. WALLER	Itom
3.	D. W. MINTER	Honda	33.	D. WEIGHTMAN	Honda (NS)
4.	M. ICHINO	Suzuki	34.	M. PETRY	Kreidler (N.S.)
5.	S. SHIMAZAKI	Honda	35.	D. P. CLARKE	D.O.T.
6.	H. G. ANSCHEIDT	Kreidler	36.	H. L. FRUIN	Fruin Dartela
7.	K. TAKAHASHI	Honda (NS)	37.	J. ASENIO	Derbi (N.S.)
8.	T. ROBB	Honda	38.	A. Dawson P/Kreidler (N.S.)	
9.	W. GEDLICH	Kreidler	39.	H. CROWDER	Kreidler
10.	L. TAVERI	Honda	40.	H. COSGROVE	Itom
11.	D. F. SHOREY	Kreidler	41.	J. D. LAWLEY	Itom
12.	M. ITOH	Suzuki	42.	S. G. W. LAWLEY	Itom
13.	T. TAKANA	Honda (NS)	43.	M. C. T. SAMPSON	Itom
14.	T. TAKANA	Honda (NS)	44.	Mrs B. J. SWAIN	Itom
15.	No nomination	M.Z. (NS)	45.	P. R. LATHAM	Itom
16.	H. Rosenbusch Tomos (N.S.)		46.	D. GUY Fruin-Dartela	Itom
17.	R. PICIGA	Tomos (N.S.)	47.	R. H. BACON	Bits
18.	M. KITANO	Honda (NS)	48.	D. A. JULER	Itom
19.	R. KUNZ	Kreidler (NS)	49.	A. J. PINK	Itom
20.	G. PARLOTTI	Tomos (N.S.)	50.	R. BRYANS	Benelli
21.	J. A. BILBAO	Derbi (N.S.)	51.	P. HARDCASTLE	Itom
22.	S. SUZUKI	Suzuki	52.	D. H. BAULCH	Itom N.S.
23.	C. G. SAMPER	Ducson N.S.	53.	G. B. BRADER	Itom
24.	J. T. HUBERTS	Kreidler	54.	Mrs B.J. SWAIN	Itom
25.	D. CHAPMAN	Kreidler N.S.	55.	P. J FOSTER	D.O.T. N.S.
26.	H. D. GERMAN	Derbi N.S.	56.	J. WRIGHT Fruin-Dart. N.S.	
27.	A DUGDALE	Benelli (NS)	57.	P. R. HORSHAM	Itom
28.	R. J. G. MAW	Itom	58.	W. D. IVY	Chisholm-Itom
29.	T. J. WOOD	Benelli (NS)			
30.	J. M. BUSQUETS	Derbi (N.S.)			

By the evening of Degner's success, fans could "read all about it" in Geoff Davison's "as it happens"-style race report in the "T.T. Special".

Degner picks up his 50 cc race trophies at the Villa Marina. The Senior Trophy and Jimmy Simpson trophy await Gary Hocking, winner of the Friday afternoon's blue riband event on his 500 cc MV. (FoTTofinders)

The 1962 TT series began disappointingly for the Suzuki boys. The 250 cc entries for Perris and Hugh Anderson were scrubbed from Monday afternoon's race, as the bikes were deemed too prone to seizure to be safe and so the TT race campaign did not get underway until the Ultra-Lightweight event held on the Wednesday morning.

The team's 125 cc challenge was virtually over before it began, with both Perris and Anderson falling by the wayside on the first of the three laps; the former was out by Ballaugh, betrayed by the seemingly inevitable seizure, while Anderson's experimental crankshaft assembly gave up the ghost on the Mountain. The third member of the team, Ernst Degner, was handicapped by under-gearing and limped home in eighth place.

But two days later came redemption, in the shape of the team's first world championship and TT victories in the inaugural 50 cc TT, courtesy of Ernst Degner. Lest it be thought that, as the race was a modest two lap affair largely populated by privateers with Itom-based "bitsas", the German's victory was hollow, it should be remembered that the contestants included the works Honda squad, the Kreidler factory's entries (including Anscheidt and Jan Huberts, the winners of the Spanish and French rounds respectively) and a host of mouth-watering combinations such as Mike Simmonds/Tohatsu, Bert Fruin on his home-made Dartela and Ralph Bryans/Benelli, and of course Beryl Swain.

"Motor Cycle" magazine went overboard in its lauding of Degner: "Fabulous! Fantastic, incredible - think of a superlative and then double it. . . .Talk about beehives. Nothing could have been buzzier than Degner's Suzuki as he flattened himself on the tank and let the revs scream up to 12,000 - the first man off in the first ever 50 cc TT."

Allocated number 2, Degner took advantage of the clear roads to establish a 15 second lead by Sulby Bridge and he completed his standing start lap in 30 m 17.8 s for a speed of 74.72 mph. Unchallenged, the second lap was completed in 29 m 58.6 s, at 75.52 mph.

The baby Suzukis proved to be reliable, with Itoh in 5th, Ichino 6th and Seichi Suzuki 8th. For good measure, Suzuki bagged the Manufacturers' Team Award and Degner would go on to take the season's 50 cc world title, as some recompense for having lost the 125 championship in the previous year.

The teamsters were jubilant with their TT victory, which signalled the breakthrough of the two-strokes and vindicated the recruitment of Degner. Although still encamped in the relatively modest surroundings of the Fernleigh, Osamu Suzuki, the president's son-in-law, celebrated by throwing a party for the squad at the upmarket Castle Mona.

And how did the press greet the two-stroke's success? The doyen of the press corps, Vic Willoughby, wrote, "Spare a thought for MZs and their boffin, Walter Kaaden, who - let's face it - developed this engine type to its present pitch in East Germany".

Willoughby was full of praise for the 50 cc steed, which had registered the first TT win by a two-stroke since 1938 when Ewald Kluge won the 250 cc race on his supercharged DKW. And Degner's winning speed was faster than that of Cromie McCandless when he won the first ever 125 cc TT on his ohc FB Mondial.

But Willoughby went on to question why the 125 cc and 250 cc models were so "outstandingly unsuccessful" - he was not pulling his punches. He concluded that Suzuki's use of aircooling, which MZ had already binned, meant that the region between the twin's cylinders was under-cooled, leading to seizures on the 250.

And Willoughby noted the hurried conversion of Degner's 125 to rear exhaust, with the fitting of an East German half-speed magneto on the rotary valve cover, in MZ mode. Ironically, it was the failure of one of the two contact-point sets - so that the engine fired only on every other revolution - that hampered Degner's efforts in the 125 race.

1963

For 1963, Suzuki had hoped to have a new square four 250 cc steed prepared for the TT but in fact the team withdrew on a temporary basis from the class, to concentrate on the two smaller categories.

The season's 50 cc model, the RM63, was merely an update of the 1962 bike, but it had gained a ninth gear and produced 11 bhp at 13,000 rpm, with a top speed of 93 mph.

By contrast, the 125 cc bike was an all new design. Designated the RT63, it was an air-cooled parallel twin cylinder affair (with rear-exhausts), measuring 43 x 42.6 mm for 123.7 cc, with a mere eight speeds. The spur was the need to improve heat dissipation by the use of smaller pistons, thereby minimising the risk of seizure. Also the engine was not as sensitive to mixture strength as 1962's single so that the rider no longer had to juggle mixture control during a race. Reliability was further enhanced by the lighter weight of the connecting rods and pistons which thereby generated lower inertia forces at high revs. Useful power was available between 11,000 rpm and 12,500 rpm with 26 bhp and 114 mph on offer. (There was also available a front exhaust version, dubbed the RT63X, which was less powerful and generally used only in non-classic events).

The Suzuki teamsters arrived in Manxland full of confidence as they had already notched up three victories in the 125 cc world title series: USA and West Germany, courtesy of Degner, and France, thanks to Hugh Anderson.

Perris on the Ultra-lightweight twin, riding to second place. (FoTTofinders)

HUGH ANDERSON

Born on 18th January 1936, New Zealander Hugh Anderson was one of a new breed of truly professional racers, an "analytical rider" in modern parlance. Having become unbeatable at home with his brace of Manx Nortons, he embarked on a European campaign in 1960 and, after sampling a couple of GPs, headed to the TT.

Hugh Anderson rounds Governor's Bridge en route to victory in the 1963 125 cc event.

He built up what he called a word picture of the daunting Mountain circuit, by scribbling page after page of notes. He recalled "It was a hell of a thrill to be there and 'Hempo' took me round in a car while I made notes about the circuit. I figured that plenty of riders before me had learned it, so why shouldn't I?"

After a couple of days, a member of the AJS race shop turned up and told him that there was a brand new 7R waiting for him . . . . courtesy of Percy Coleman. Eschewing the well-worn theory that three years were needed to learn the circuit, after a mere eight laps of practising, Anderson registered fifth fastest time. He was advised to restrain himself; indeed his new mates Bob Brown and Dickie Dale told him to never forget the next meeting. "It was a good thing to remember during a race - it could stop you getting hurt." Meanwhile, Coleman was busy trying to get insurance on the 7R!

In eighth place after the second lap of the Junior TT, a broken valve spring brought his efforts to a premature conclusion at Union Mills just into the next lap. But he had undoubtedly made his mark.

As for a works ride, Anderson claimed, somewhat cryptically, " I always felt a works ride would come if I was good enough. I didn't chase any team - unlike some." Thanks to Lew Ellis, Anderson had the choice of Suzuki and Bianchi rides for the 1961 TT and, by opting for the Japanese team, the die was cast.

A full Suzuki contract came for 1962, along with rides for Tom Arter on experimental AJS and Matchless racers, and Anderson was on the path to no fewer than 25 GP victories and four world titles - the 50 cc and 125 cc double in 1963, the 50 cc title in the following year and finally the 125 cc title in 1965.

By his own admission, he was a one-off; his mechanical expertise, his paperwork and long hours burning the midnight oil in the garage with his mechanics distinguished him from many of his peers; he forsook the party-loving style of many of his rivals and team-mates and embraced an endurance and aerobic fitness regime, running three miles a day and carrying out daily press-ups and sit-ups.

At the end of 1966, his ambitions on the tarmac fulfilled, he walked away from the circus and switched to off-road events, both grass track and moto-cross. In the 1970s, he took up classic racing and has been an avid participant in racing and parading ever since then, with a return to the TT in the Lap of Honour in 2005 exhibiting another Kiwi legend, the fabulous vee-twin Britten.

The TT series began embarrassingly on the Monday of race week when the squad of Anderson, Perris, Degner and Schneider was withdrawn from the Lightweight TT as the new 250 cc square four, the RZ63, was still in the course of preparation but well behind schedule - and indeed it did not appear until the season's final GP, the Japanese - which proved to be a disaster when Degner was the victim of an explosion when the petrol tank blew up after a heavy crash, suffering injuries which put him out of action for a year.

Bertie Schneider astride the 125 cc machine. Born in Vienna on 28 August 1936, Schneider sadly passed away on 2 July 2009, just before this book went to press.

But redemption came two days later when those same riders notched first, second, third and fifth positions respectively in the three lap Ultra-Lightweight TT, humiliating the strong Honda team and of course picking up the Manufacturers' Prize. Mist and drizzle delayed the start but, once away, Anderson was untroubled by the competition. His sole problem was negotiating the dreaded mist on the Mountain, clouting the bank at the Black Hut and riding into the verges on a couple of occasions thanks to the reduced visibility.

On the final lap, thanks to dry roads, despite being under-geared and suffering from over-jetting denying him 200 rpm, he took the lap record up to 24 m 47.4 s (89.27 mph) - although he was denied the race record by the mist and damp roads of the first half hour.

Two days later, another Suzuki victory was virtually assured, as the six strong squad's only "works" opposition was posed by

Post-125 cc race and the Suzuki squad celebrates its clean sweep: Degner, Anderson and Perris. To the right, scribe Willoughby scribbles his notes in readiness for his race report in "Motor Cycle" magazine. (FoTTofinders)

FRIDAY, 14th JUNE

50 c.c. INTERNATIONAL—3 LAPS
113.2 Miles
The race will start at 11.00 a.m. and the competitors will be despatched in pairs at intervals as shown.

No.	Driver	Machine	Start Interval M. S.	1st Lap	2nd Lap	3rd Lap
1	B. Schneider (Austria)	50 Suzuki	00 00			
2	H. G. Anscheidt (W. Germany)	50 Kreidler	00 00			
3	A. Pagani (Italy)	50 Kreidler	00 10			
4	H. R. Anderson (New Zealand)	50 Suzuki	00 10			
* 5	E. Degner (W. Germany)	50 Suzuki	00 20			
6	R. Torras (Spain)	50 Kreidler	00 20			
7	J. Huberts (Holland)	50 N.N.	00 30			
8	M. Itoh (Japan)	50 Suzuki	00 30			
9	R. Avery	49 Derbi	00 40			
10	M. Ichino (Japan)	50 Suzuki	00 40			
†11			00 50			
12		50 Kreidler	00 50			
14	I. Morishita (Japan)	50 Suzuki	01 00			
15	J. M. Busquets (Spain)	49 Derbi	01 10			
16	M. J. Simmonds	49 Tohatsu	01 10			
17	R. Bryans (Ireland)	50 Honda	01 20			
18	J. Asensio (Spain)	49 Derbi	01 20			
19	H. Crowder	50 Kreidler	01 30			
20	W. D. Ivy	49 Derbi	01 30			
†21			01 40			
22	C. C. W. Mates	50 Suzuki	01 40			
23	D. A. Simmonds	49 Tohatsu	01 50			
24	C. Gracia (Spain)	49 Derbi	01 50			
25	P. R. Latham	50 Suzuki	02 00			
26	D. A. Juler	50 Itom	02 00			
27	H. L. Fruin	50 Fruin Dartela	02 10			
28	P. J. Foster	47 Dot	02 10			
29	A. J. Pink	50 Honda	02 20			
30	A. E. Dawson	50 Pope Special	02 20			
31	A. F. Roth (Switzerland)	50 Tohatsu	02 30			
32	P. Eser (W. Germany)	50 Honda	02 30			
33	D. Armstrong	50 Itom	02 40			
34	A. G. Hutchings	49 Benelli	02 40			
35	B. Smith (Australia)	50 Itom	02 50			
36	I. E. Plumridge	50 Val Knapp Honda	02 50			
37	B. C. Goldthorp	49 C.G.S. Special	03 00			

* Denotes previous winner of 50 c.c. T.T. Race.
† Numbers retained by A.C.U. for re-allocation.

Scorecard for the 50 cc TT, 14 June 1963. Itoh's victory remains the only TT success by a Japanese rider.

Itoh takes his tiddler (or "wasp" as Geoff Davison described the' fifties) around Quarter Bridge.

Ichino and Morishita round Governor's Bridge; they finished 5th and 4th respectively in "Itoh's race".

the Kreidlers of Georg Anscheidt and Alberto Pagani. Certainly the Kreidler boys, making full use of their twelve speeds, made a spectacular challenge during the first of the three laps - Anscheidt passed Anderson in mid-air across Ballaugh Bridge while Pagani and Degner joined in an on-the-roads battle.

Sadly, Pagani had his plug go sour on the Mountain although his German team-mate had the lead at Keppel Gate. But down the Mountain the higher top speed of the Japanese machines began to tell and, on corrected time, Degner had a narrow lead from Itoh - and the first six had cracked the existing lap record.

The second lap saw speeds mount, with the first five all within the new lap record, Anscheidt still in with chance of spoiling the Suzuki monopoly and Suzuki's newcomer Isao Morishita clouting the bank on the exit from Signpost.

Drama on lap three as Mitsuo Itoh, starting at number 8, caught Degner on the road at Glen Helen, to take the lead on corrected time and sweep past him on the fast drop at Barregarrow. Degner was suffering ignition problems while Anscheidt, still leading on the roads, had suspension bothers - so Itoh screamed by as they climbed the Mountain.

As Itoh took the chequered fag to become the first, and to date, only Japanese winner of a TT, Degner finally retired at the Waterworks. The other Suzuki finishers were Anderson (2nd), Morishita (4th) and Ichino (5th) - complete with rags round the filler caps to soak up leaking petroil. (Schneider joined Degner as a retirement).

Isao Morishita rounds Quarter Bridge on his RM63.

FIRST-EVER T.T. WIN FOR JAPANESE RIDER

Itoh's Dramatic Victory in 50 c.c. Race

By GEOFF DAVISON

HISTORY was made for the T.T. today when Mitsu Itoh became the first Japanese rider ever to win one of the coveted trophies.

In a dramatic last lap of the record breaking 50 c.c. race Ernst Degner the pace setter and leader went out of the running and Itoh's Suzuki came home to victory at a record 78.81 m.p.h.

Record lap was set up by Degner's Suzuki at 79.10 m.p.h.

The Press Box, Friday.

This morning's "Wasp" race is only the second of the series, so there isn't much "history" to write about. It is due to start at 11 a.m., and it has attracted an entry of 34, as against 57 last year. This is rather disappointing, but there are some obvious reasons for it. Last year, for instance, there were fifteen Itoms amongst the entries, but they just weren't fast enough to stand a chance against the Japs and the Germans.

The best Itom finished 16th, at 58.65 m.p.h. against the winner's speed of 75.12 m.p.h. So this year there are only three Itoms . . . the "Gerjap" supremacy had made many riders think that it's a waste of time to come over here and fight a losing battle.

Then again the "Financial Assistance" offered to the Fifties was £10 a-piece, against £15 each for riders in the other solo races. Why? It costs as much on the boat for a 50 c.c. model as for a "500" — and the riders don't get reduced boarding house or hotel bills just because they are racing such very small machines . . .

And another thing—they have only been allotted three half-period practices, as against five full periods for the 125's and 250's, and seven full periods for for the Juniors and Seniors. What with one thing and another a large entry was not exactly "encouraged." It is to be hoped that the Fifties will get a better deal next year. I leave that thought with the Auto-Cycle Union . . .

Last year's two lap race was won by Ernst Degner (Suzuki) at 75.12 m.p.h., and Degner established the lap record at 75.52. In practice this year Degner has (unofficially) beaten his last year's record with a lap at 79.06 m.p.h., and four other riders have improved on the 75.52.

On the Sulby Mile, Hugh Anderson clocked 90 m.p.h. in practice against last year's best of 86.97 m.p.h. The "Wasps" are certainly going some.

The 34 entries are composed of eight Suzukis, five Kreidlers, four Derbis and four Hondas, three Itoms and three Tohatsus, and one each Benelli, C.G.S., D.O.T., Fruin-Dartela, "N.N." Pope-Special and Sheene Special. Japan leads with 17 entries, and Germany comes next with five.

An element of "gloom" is caused by the fact that there are 16 non-starters — as shown on the list at the top of this page — reducing the field to 18. Amongst these there is one four-stroke single (Plumridge's Honda), 16 two-stroke singles, and one two stroke twin (D. A. Simmonds' Tohatsu). It's a practically certain win for a two-stroke, and most probably a "single."

B. Schneider (Suzuki) and H. G. Anscheidt (Kreidler) are due off the mark at 11 a.m., and the last man away, at ten seconds before 11.3 a.m. will be Plumridge on the only four-stroke. They have to do three laps — 113.2 miles — as in the "curtain raisers" of Monday and Wednesday.

The 7.55 a.m. weather forecast spoke of "some hill fog" early on, conditions improving later with some sunshine this afternoon. The Ronaldsway "Met." report at 9 a.m. was not so good, though — "cloud affecting the mountain section of the course, probably clearing in the early afternoon; winds light and variable. roads damp as a result of overnight rain, but drying as the day progresses."

Still it's not too bad up here — the outline of the Mountain is just visible, and there seems to be no likelihood of postponement.

10.30 a.m. — the warm-up period starts, and the "Wasps" are buzzing up and down the tarmac strip. It's quite cool, and there should be no trouble from wet tar on the roads, as there was on Monday.

There are two Manufacturers' Teams, Suzuki 'A' with Anderson Degner and Itoh, and Suzuki 'B' (Schneider, Ichino and Morishita); there is only one club team though — the Racing "50" M.C.C. with M. J. Simmonds, D. A. Simmonds and I. E. Plumridge.

10.40 — silence on the tarmac, five minutes before the official signal ; the Wasps are warm enough ! But as I write the words some of them get going again, for a last minute try-out.

10.45 — The Maroon; the 18 riders wheel their machines on to the starting grids. Owing to the weather conditions, with unfavourable winds on the Mountein, Ernst Degner, last year's winner has fitted a new rear sprocket, one tooth smaller.

10.55 a.m.—the Five Minute Maroon. Four minutes, three minutes, two minutes, one minute — and Schneider and Anscheidt are away; Schneider is quicker off the mark than his "time-mate". M. J. Simmonds (Tohatsu) is rather a slow starter but his motor takes it as he passes the pits

All get away well, and at 11.3 a.m. there is silence at the start.

Hugh Anderson (Suzuki—No. 4) is first at Ballacraine, Anscheidt (Kreidler—No. 2) is there next, followed by Degner (No. 5) and Pagani (No. 3)—all within five seconds.

News from Crosby — Bert Schneider (Suzuki—No. 1) has stopped there and is making adjustments.

At Bishop's Court Anderson is still leading on the roads followed by No. 2 (Anscheidt), No. 5 (Degner), No. 8 (Itoh) and No. 3 (Pagani). The order is the same at Ballaugh, and at Ramsey

The first retirement — Bert Schneider, previously reported as making adjustments at Crosby.

ENTRIES IN THE 50 c.c. RACE

1. B. SCHNEIDER .... Suzuki
2. H. G. ANSCHEIDT ...... Kreidler
3. A. PAGANI .... Kreidler
4. H. ANDERSON .... Suzuki
5. E. DEGNER .... Suzuki
6. R. TORRAS .... Kreidler (NS)
7. J. HUBERTS .... N.N. (NS)
8. M. ITOH .... Suzuki
9. R. AVERY .... Derbi (NS)
10. M. ICHINO .... Suzuki
11. No Nomination
12. .... Kreidler (NS)
14. I. MORISHITA .... Suzuki
15. J. M. BUSQUETS Derbi (NS)
16. M. J. SIMMONDS .. Tohatsu
17. R. BRYANS ...... Honda (NS)
18. J. ASENSIO .... Derbi (NS)
19. H. CROWDER .... Kreidler
20. W. D. IVY ... Sheene Special
21. No Nomination.
22. C. W. MATES .. Suzuki (NS)
23. D. A. SIMMONDS Tohatsu
24. C. GRACIA ..... Derbi (NS)
25. P. R. LATHAM Suzuki (NS)
26. D. A. JULER .... Itom
27. H. L. FRUIN Fruin Dartela
28. P. J. FOSTER .... Dot
29. A. J. PINK ...... Honda (NS)
30. A. E. DAWSON .... Pope Sp.
31. A. F. ROTH Tohatsu (NS)
32. P. ESER .... Honda (NS)
33. D. ARMSTRONG Itom (NS)
34. A. G. HUTCHINGS .. Benelli
35. B. SMITH ...... Itom (NS)
36. I. E. PLUMRIDGE ... Honda
37. B. Goldthorp CGS Sp. (NS)

MITSUO ITOH pilots his Suzuki at Signpost to score the all-Japanese 50 c.c. win

has packed it in there; out goes Suzuki "B" team.

Anscheidt has overtaken Anderson on the Mountain climb, and is leading him at the Bungalow with Degner third on the roads (No. 8) and Itoh a good fourth.

Another retirement — A. G. Hutchings (Benelli) at Selborne Drive with engine trouble, rider O.K. of course. Only 16 left.

Now the first four are all shown at Signpost Corner, and here they are past the pits. Anscheidt is about ten yards in front of Anderson, Degner is three seconds behind the leader and Itoh (No. 8), is some 13 seconds back; this gives both of them several seconds lead on corrected time.

Three more retirements, all riders O.K. — Pagani at the Bungalow, H. Crowder (Kreidler) at Laurel Bank, and D. A. Simmonds (Tohatsu) at Crosby — so out goes the one Club Team.

FIRST LAP LEADERS

	m. s.
E. Degner (Suzuki) (78.46 m.p.h.)	28 51.2
M. Itoh (Suzuki) (78.43 m.p.h.)	28 51
H. Anderson (Suzuki) (78.09 m.p.h.)	28 59.4
H. G. Anscheidt (Kreidler) (77.65 m.p.h.)	29 9.2
I. Morishita (Suzuki) (77.06 m.p.h.)	29 22.6
M. Ichino (Suzuki) (76.19 m.p.h.)	29 4.8

Degner's lap, from a standing start, is a new record for the race, and the first six have ALL beaten the existing record !

At Barregarrow on the second lap Degner is leading on the roads, followed by Anscheidt and Anderson.

P. J. Foster (DOT) has retired at Cruickshank's Corner, O.K.

The first three on the roads— Degner, Anderson and Anscheidt —keep on swopping positions, first one and then another take the lead; but at the Mountain it's a case of Degner, Anderson, Anscheidt, with No. 8 Itoh. not far behind—and it's the same at Hillberry.

11.58 a.m.—here they are past the pits — Degner, Anderson, Anscheidt, separted only by a few yards Itoh comes past some 13 seconds later, which means that he has dropped back a little on Degner.

SECOND LAP LEADERS

	m. s.
E. Degner (Suzuki) (78.79 m.p.h.)	57 28.4
F. Itoh (Suzuki) (78.72 m.p.h.)	57 31
H. Anderson (Suzuki) (78.54 m.p.h.)	57 39
H. Anscheidt (Kreidler) (78.32 m.p.h.)	57 49.2
I. Morishita (Suzuki) (77.80 m.p.h.)	58 12
M. Ichino (Suzuki) (76.29 m.p.h.)	59 21.4

Suzukis still in the first three places . . . and in fifth and sixth as well.

H. L. Fruin coasts in and retires at the pits. A. E. Dawson (Pope Special) has retired at Cronk-y-voddy, O.K.

Kirk Michael reports that the order past there is Anscheidt, Anderson. Itoh, Degner. This means that Degner has dropped back and that Itoh is leading the race!

12.10 p.m.—there are now eight retirements and only ten runners on the course—other than the Travelling Marshals, of course.

Sulby reports that Degner is "touring"—bad luck Ernst.

The first four men on the second lap leader board have all taken the new lap record, and Degner has raised it to 79.10 m.p.h—28 mins. 37.2 secs.

At Guthrie's on the last lap Itoh has increased his lead on Anscheidt and Anderson, and position is the same at the Mountain Box.

12.25 p.m. (approx)—the three leaders on the roads are shown at Signpost, and now here comes M. Itoh to win the 50 c.c. race and to score the first all-Japanese T.T. victory.

Ernst Degner is now announced as having retired with engine trouble at the Waterworks, so the Suzukis 'A' team is out of it.

RESULT

	h. m. s.
1. M. Itoh (Suzuki) (78.81 m.p.h.)	1 26 10.6
2. H. Anderson (Suzuki) (78.40 m.p.h.)	1 26 37.4
3. H. G. Anscheidt (Kreidler) (78.33 m.p.h.)	1 26 42
4. I. Morishita (Suzuki) (77.82 m.p.h.)	1 27 16
5. M. Inchino (Suzuki) (76.20 m.p.h.)	1 29 7.6
6. I. E. Plumridge (Honda) (64.82 m.p.h.)	1 44 46.4
7. W. D. Ivy (Sheene Spl.) (61.12 m.p.h.)	1 51 7.2
8. M. J. Simmonds (Tohatsu) (54.02 m.p.h.)	2 5 44

completed two laps

| D. A. Juler (Itom) (46.37 m.p.h.) | 1 37 39 |

H. ANDERSON (Suzuki) in action in today's 50 c.c. T.T.

The same day "T.T. Special" records the Itoh-Suzuki win. . . .

MOTOR CYCLE 20 JUNE 1963

All-Japanese

MITSUO ITOH (SUZUKI) WINS 50 c.c. T.T.
DEGNER HOISTS THE LAP RECORD TO OVER 79 m.p.h.

WITH six Suzukis against two Kreidlers in the 50 c.c. Race the chances of a Suzuki win seemed more than just a possibility—it was a cert, or darned nearly so. But the sheer guts which Georg Anscheidt (Kreidler) displayed as he took on the Suzuki lads single handed, after team-mate Alberto Pagani retired on the first lap, set fire to a race which beforehand seemed likely to be more of a smoulder. There were only 18 starters out of 33 entries with not even a woman among them for added interest.

One could hardly have expected an exciting spectacle. Yet that is precisely what the leaders provided as Anscheidt and Alberto Pagani, Hugh Anderson and Ernst Degner (Suzuki) swarmed together on the road, frantically trying to outdo one another on every corner.

The enterprising Anscheidt even tried passing Anderson in mid-air across Ballaugh Bridge—and he did too! But Pagani had his plug go sour on the mountain, pushed to the Bungalow and, later, toured in. This left Anscheidt to take on the Suzuki team and he loved every yard of it.

standing start! How about that for winter development?

Less than a minute covered the first six at the end of that lap. Degner's lead over team-mate Mitsuo Itoh was a mere 0.6s! Anderson was 7.6s behind Itoh, with Anscheidt a further 9.8s astern. But Georg had a luxurious 13.4s in hand over newcomer Isao Morishito (Suzuki). Last of the Suzuki runners, was Michio Ichino, just 20.2s astern of his team.

All this rather overshadowed the remainder of the field—and no wonder. Seventh man Ian Plumridge, on his production o.h.c. Honda—only four-stroke in the race—was trailing 5m 28.6s behind the sixth man!

Up the strenuous Mountain climb, he played just the right tune on his 12 ratios and had a clear 100-yd lead by Keppel Gate. But down the other side, the Suzukis showed the advantage of their extra speed and Anderson was right on Anscheidt's tail past the grand-stand.

Degner was some 100 yards behind, but from the manner in which he belted along the Glencrutchery Road, he obviously meant business.

It was no surprise that Degner's first lap was a record—no less than 1m 7.4s off his previous best, made last year. Even more startling, *the first six all handsomely cracked last year's record*—and this from a

MOTOR CYCLE 20 JUNE 1963

Harry Crowder dropped his home-brewed Kreidler at Laurel Bank, but was unhurt. After a very slow first lap, attributed to clutch slip, jumping out of gear, pre-ignition and seizure, Bert Fruin (Fruin Dürch) coasted to the pits.

All the way round that second lap the leading trio swopped positions corner by corner. On the approach to Keppel, Anderson dived past Degner in a vain attempt to shake off the determined Anscheidt. But on the climb to Cronk-ny-Mona, Anscheidt pulled up again.

At Signpost, the two Suzuki men sat up and braked. Anscheidt dished his anchors. Fifth man, Morishito, sat up and slammed on his anchors. But Georg clouted the bank coming out of Signpost and almost gave himself and the spectators heart failure.

Fabulous! As second-lap times were posted the first-lap order remained unchanged and the first five men had all broken the next lap record!

By Glen Helen on the third and last lap, Degner was again in front, with Anderson on his tail and Anscheidt still right there with them. But creeping up on this trio was Itoh.

Only 100 yards behind Glen Helen, he swept past Degner—now third on the road—on the very fast drop at Barregarrow to snatch the lead.

Poor Degner! By Sulby Bridge, he had shot his bolt and dropped right back with ignition trouble. Suspension bothers had given Anscheidt some anxious moments, so he eased the pace and Itoh whistled by as they screamed up the Mountain.

As Itoh sat up and grinned at the chequered flag—the first-ever all-Japanese T.T. win—Degner limped to Water-works and there retired.

Down Bray Hill winner Mitsuo Itoh (Suzuki) is jolted off his seat.

Average speed of the first five was handsomely above last year's lap record. That meant that sixth man and first private runner, Ian Plumridge, was not fast enough to qualify even for a bronze replica.

					m.p.h.
1	M. ITOH (SUZUKI)	1	26	10.6	78.31
2	H. ANDERSON (SUZUKI)	1	26	37.4	78.40
3	H. E. ANSCHEIDT (KREIDLER)	1	26	42.0	78.33
4	I. Morishito (Suzuki)	1	27	16.2	77.81
5	M. Ichino (Suzuki)	1	29	07.6	76.20
6	I. E. Plumridge (Valkapp Honda)	1	44	45.4	64.82
7	W. D. Ivy (Sheene Special)	2	05	44.8	51.02
8	M. J. Simmonds (Tohatsu)				

Fastest-Lap—Degner, 28m 37.2s, 79.1 m.p.h. (record). First-class Replica—Nos. 1 to 5 inclusive (time limit: 1h 36m 57s). Second-class Replica (time limit: 1h 43m 24.6s). No team finished intact.

Battling Georg Anscheidt (Kreidler) chases Suzuki speedsters Ernst Degner—that's the lap-record holder in the lead—and Hugh Anderson round Creg-ny-Baa. Mitsuo Itoh is dropping down from Kate's Cottage

. . . and next week's "Motor Cycle" applauds the all-Japanese success.

1964

For the 1964 season, the 50 cc model, the RM64, had a shorter stroke than its predecessor, allowing increased rpm and 12.5 bhp at 14,000 rpm, but was otherwise similar. Likewise, the 125 cc RT64 was little changed from the 1963 bike.

But the big news was that the square four 250 was apparently ready, a theory seemingly proved by its performance in practice

1964 saw the much-anticipated first appearance of Whispering Death in the Isle of Man. Here Perris is seen at Quarter Bridge.

at Daytona for the US GP. Perris recalled: "Bertie and I were riding together when we came upon a large red bike. It was Hailwood on the 500 MV and we caught and passed him quite easily."

However, it was one thing for the square four to perform respectably on the ultra fast banking at Daytona and another altogether on twisty circuits over which handling was at a premium.

A series of seizures in testing and unspectacular performances in the Spanish and French title rounds led to Anderson refusing to ride the 250 and so, at the suggestion of Perris and Schneider, Jack Ahearn was approached.

Ahearn was a 39 year old Australian whose career had taken off when he bought, off Ken Kavanagh, what was reputedly an ex-works Norton which Kavanagh had taken Down Under at the end of 1951. Ahearn was selected as Australia's representative for the 1954 TT and so began a career as a prominent member of the Continental Circus during the 'fifties. A three year absence from Europe, while he built a house in Sydney and drove taxis to finance his racing, put him out of contention for a works ride.

Practice shot of Schneider on the evil 250. . . (Walter Radcliffe collection)

. . . . which threw him off at Ramsey hairpin on race day (Walter Radcliffe collection)

But by 1964 Jack was riding well and indeed he would finish the season as runner-up to Hailwood in the 500 cc world championship. And, in Ahearn's words, "Suzuki were looking for someone with a small brain and a big right hand to ride that 250 - and that was me."

Alas, the 250 cc TT was another humbling experience for the four cylinder model. Perris reached no further than the Highlander on lap one. Ahearn and Schneider finished the first lap in sixth and seventh places, a minute behind the leader (and eventual winner) Redman. Schneider dropped the multi at Ramsey hairpin on lap two and, eventually managing to start the plot pushing uphill, suffered a broken chain as he swept down to the Creg. Ahearn got to the Highlander for the third time but no further.

Two days later came the 125 cc event, which turned out to be almost as bad for the team. Starting alongside Taveri on one of the new four cylinder Hondas, Anderson passed him at Union Mills, over-revved and immediately knew that he was in trouble. A mile later, the engine locked solid. Schneider was another to go out with a dead engine on the first of the three laps, leaving Perris to carry the challenge. The lone Suzuki did so to great effect on the first lap, trailing leader Redman by a mere 0.2 seconds. But the Suzuki engine cried enough on lap two and he could do no more than limp back to the pits to retire, leaving Taveri, Redman and Bryans to register a Honda 1-2-3.

But the 50 cc race brought consolation when Anderson had a record-breaking unchallenged run to victory, with team mates Morishita and Itoh in third and fifth, and Koshino the sole team retirement.

A postscript was that, for the remainder of the season, Ahearn was offered further rides on the 250 four but it was a mixed blessing - it constantly threw him off, causing him to christen it, memorably, "Whispering Death."

Quarter Bridge again features as the backdrop for Jack Ahearn astride the ill-tempered square four 250.

A marvellous shot of Ahearn and his 250 at Creg-ny-Baa.

Hugh Anderson awaits the start of the 1964 125 cc event. . . .

. . . .and has the soles of his boots checked prior to the start of the 50 cc race two days later.

The Kiwi star taking his RM64 to victory. . . .

12   *"Examiner" T.T. Special, Friday, 12th June, 1964*

ANDERSON'S 80 M.P.H. 50 c.c. VICTORY

SUZUKI LAPS COURSE AT 81.13 M.P.H.

By GEOFF DAVISON

HUGH ANDERSON, from New Zealand, took the 50 c.c. Suzuki round the Mountain Course today at 80.64 m.p.h. for three laps — and at 81.13 for one lap — to set up new records in his great victory in the "baby" T.T. of the week.

It was a triumph for Suzuki, with Morishita in third place, Ralph Bryan's Honda clinching runner-up award with a superb last lap.

The Press Box.

The "Wasps" are due as the Curtain Raisers to today's events. They have to cover three laps of the T.T. Mountain Course, as they did last year, and will be started at 10-second intervals.

Unfortunately the entries are down again this year—only 28 of them, as against 35 last year and 56 in 1962. But, with the notable exception of Lap Record breaker, Ernest Degner, most of the "fast men" are there.

Degner's lap speed last year was 79.10 m.p.h.—time, 28 mins. 37.2 secs. No one came within 16.8 seconds of this in this year's practices. Mitsuo Itoh (Suzuki), who won the race last year after Degner had retired, having scored a lap in 28 mins 54 secs., at 78.35 m.p.h.

HUGH ANDERSON on his record-breaking Suzuki in today's 50 c.c. T.T.

there, with the exception of Huberts and Tommy Robb, of course. In addition to the six fastest in practice, H. G. Anscheidt and Tarquinio Provini (Kreidlers) may well figure on the race Leader Board, as may the Tohatsus driven by the Simmonds brothers.

Last year, out of 36 entries there were 18 non-starters, making a field of 18 only. So in spite of the reduced entry **WE'RE TWO-UP-ON-THE-ROADS TODAY.**

Incidentally, for the record, we timed the "Wasps" over the first mile of the T.T. course, from the starting line to a point just beyond Selborne Drive, on the Quarter Bridge Road. We got them with both standing and flying starts. The fastest "standers" were H. Koshino (Suzuki) and N. Taniguchi (Honda) at 70.59 m.p.h., and the quickest flyers were the following:—

		m.p.h.
1. I. Morishita	(Suzuki)	94.74
2. N. Taniguchi	(Honda)	92.31
3. H. R. Anderson	(Suzuki)	90.00
3. L. Taveri	(Kreidler)	90.00
5. H. Koshino	(Suzuki)	87.81
6. M. Simmonds	(Tohatsu)	77.93

During its mile, the stretch drops about 150 feet, but even so 94.74 m.p.h. isn't so bad for a "50"!

Anscheidt and Koshino are due off at 11 a.m., and the last man, R. J. Smith, should leave at 20 seconds after 11.2 a.m. Hugh Anderson starts 10 seconds after the first pair, and Bryans, Morishita and Taveri leave 20, 30 and 40 seconds, respectively, after the first couple. Most of the riders are on two-strokes, of course.

The weather yesterday was lovely, but there was obviously sea mist during the night for "Moaning Mona", the Douglas fog-horn, was at it all the time.

It wasn't too bad when I first took a look at it at about 7-30 a.m. and the 7-55 a.m. forecast was hopeful — "cloudy at first in the Isle of Man, with perhaps a little rain later, mainly dry with sunny periods; light or moderate south to south east wind, warm."

10-30 a.m.—the warm-up maroon. The weather is O.K.

These are three Manufacturers' Teams—European Honda, Kreidler and Suzuki—but only one Club Team, that of the Racing 50 M.C.C., of which I have the honour to be President!

10-40 a.m.—"Visibility on the Mountain is half-a-mile and it's clearing." Good news. And it's really quite warm—for a change! —in the Press Box.

The "possible winners" are well spread out in the first twenty. I make it that there are nearly a dozen of them, running from No. 1, H. G. Anscheidt to No. 20, Provini, both on Kreidlers.

10-45 a.m.—the maroon to stop engines—but actually they had

Koshino (No. 2) is shown at all stopped two or three minutes ago.

10-50 am.—the sun is almost shining, and the outline of the Mountain is now quite clear. Conditions all round the course should be ideal.

10-55 a.m.—the Five Minute Maroon. Four minues, three, two, one.

11 a.m.—Anscheidt and Koshino are away, with the Jap leading on the approach to St. Ninian's.

All get away all right, but Taveri has to push quite a long way before the model takes it. and Provini is slower than most; odd, that!

creasing his lead. The order then is Koshino (2), Anscheidt (1), Bryans (5), Morishita (7) and Itoh (18). Anderson is first on the roads and in the race, and it seems that Morishita and Itoh are running second and third.

11.28 a.m.—approx.—here come the first three at the end of lap 1, and it is Anscheidt who is now leading on the roads! But Anderson has got in front again at Quarter Bridge.

No. 18, last year's winner. Itoh —is now running sixth on the roads.

Hugh Anderson has broken the lap record from a standing start, with a time of 28 mins. 24.4 secs. at 79.69 m.p.h. He may well beat the "four-score" on second flying start lap. Itoh, Anscheidt and Koshino have also beaten last year's record!

FIRST LAP LEADERS

		m. s.
1. H. Anderson	(Suzuki)	28 24.4
	(79.69 m.p.h.)	
2. M. Itoh	(Suzuki)	28 32.8
	(79.30 m.p.h.)	
3. H. Anscheidt	(Krd'l)	28 33.6
	(79.26 m.p.h.)	
4. H. Koshino	(Suzuki)	28 34.4
	(79.23 m.p.h.)	
5. I. Morishita	(Suzuki)	28.41.6
	(78.90 m.p.h.)	
6. N. Taniguchi	(Honda)	28 48.4
	(78.59 m.p.h.)	

So Hugh Anderson had a lead of 8.4 seconds on his team-mate Mitsuo Itoh, who is less than a second ahead of Anscheidt—four Suzukis in the first five!

The first retirement—R. J. Smith (Honda) at Glen Vine with engine trouble rider O.K., of course.

11.52 a.m.—All quiet at the Grandstand—the first six on the roads have passed the Bungalow.

Another retirement—Jim Pink (Honda) has come off at Ramsey, is quite O.K. but has had to pack it in—bad luck, Jim.

11.55 a.m.—Hugh Anderson is at Signpost Corner, and now he's here, about half a minute ahead (on the roads) of Anscheidt and Koshino. It is nearly two minutes before Itoh arrives, so Hugh has obviously increased his lead.

And he has broken the "four-score", with a second lap at 81.10 m.p.h.— time, 27 mins. 54.8 secs!

12.5 p.m.—Hugh Anderson has passed Barregarrow for the last time—and now he's at Kirk Michael.

News that M. J. Simmonds (Tohatsu) has come off at Waterworks—unhurt. but retired.

12.13 p.m.—Hugh Anderson is shown at Ramsey — barring accidents "it's in the bag".

SECOND LAP LEADERS

		m. s.
1. H. R. Anderson	(Suzuki)	56 19.2
	(80.39 m.p.h.)	
2. H. G. Anscheidt	(Kreidler)	56 55.6
	(79.53 m.p.h.)	
3. H. Koshino	(Suzuki)	56 56.6
	(79.51 m.p.h.)	
4. M. Itoh	(Suzuki)	57 02
	(79.38 m.p.h.)	
5. I. Morishita	(Suzuki)	57 04.6
	(79.32 m.p.h.)	
6. R. Bryans	(Honda)	57 08.2
	(79.24 m.p.h.)	

7th N. Taniguchi (Honda), 8th, L. Taveri (Kreidler); 9th T. Provini (Kreidler); 10th D. A. Simmonds (Tohatsu); 11th L. E. Plumridge (Honda) and 12th P. Horsham (Honda).

So Anscheidt has pulled up into second place. Japan's machinery takes all the first six places except the second, where Germany comes in.

12.19 p.m.—Hugh is at the Bungalow—only about seven miles to go. Anscheidt is shown at the Bungalow about a minute later.

12-23—Hugh is shown at Signpost, and here he comes past to win the 1964 "Wasp" race by a substantial margin.

Anscheidt is along next, but Ralph Bryans a quarter of a minute after him, which means a lead of four seconds on corrected time.

Another retirement — C. C. Mates at Ramsey, O.K.

Now comes news of Hugh's times. His last lap was done in 27 mins. 54.2 secs., at the new record speed of 81.13 m.p.h., and he has won the race at over the "four-score" — 80.64 m.p.h.

Great excitement! — Ralph Bryans, lying sixth on the second lap, has drawn up into second place, with Morishita there and Anscheidt fourth.

News of Koshino—he came off near Brandywell, and has been seen by a doctor, who reports that there is "nothing broken".

After his victory, Hugh Anderson told our reporter of how his engine started missing on the Mountain during the first lap, which enabled Anscheidt to lead on the roads at the end of the lap. Otherwise everything went alright.

FINAL LAP LEADERS

		h. m. s.
1. H. R. Anderson	(Suzuki)	1 24 13.4
	(80.64 m.p.h.)	
2. R. Bryans	(Honda)	1 25 14.8
	(79.68 m.p.h.)	
3. I. Morishita	(Suzuki)	1 25 15.4
	(79.67 m.p.h.)	
4. H. G. Anscheidt	(Kreidler)	1 25 18
	(79.63 m.p.h.)	
5. M. Itoh	(Suzuki)	1 25 22.4
	(79.57 m.p.h.)	
6. N. Taniguchi	(Honda)	1 25 33
	(79.39 m.p.h.)	
7. L. Taveri	(Kreidler)	1 26 27.4
	(78.56 m.p.h.)	
8. T. Provini	(Kreidler)	1 30 39.6
	(74.92 m.p.h.)	

(all above receive silver replicas)

9. D. A. Simmonds	(Tohatsu)	1 36 18
	(70.53 m.p.h.)	
10. L. E. Plumridge	(Honda)	1 39 08.8
	(68.51 m.p.h.)	
11. P. Horsham	(Honda)	1 39 21.2
	(68.37 m.p.h.)	

(all above receive bronze replicas)

12. J. Tompsett	(Honda)	1 44 30.4
	(65 m.p.h.)	
13. L. E. Evans	(Honda)	1 44 51.4
	(64.78 m.p.h.)	
14. A. G. Hutchins	(Honda)	1 48 01.2
	(62.88 m.p.h.)	
15. D. A. Juler	(Itom)	1 59 45.8
	(56.72 m.p.h.)	

Manufacturers prize: Suzuki (Anderson, Morishita and Itoh).

RUNNER-UP in today's 50 c.c. T.T. — Ralph Bryans (Honda).

Still, the first half dozen fastest in Practice all lapped in under the half-hour, as shown below:—

	m. s.
M. Itoh (Suzuki)	28 54
(78.35 m.p.h.)	
R. Bryans (Honda)	28 57.6
(78.18 m.p.h.)	
H. R. Anderson (Suzuki)	29 03.2
(77.93 m.p.h.)	
I. Morishita (Suzuki)	29 06
(77.81 m.p.h.)	
N. Taniguchi (Honda)	29 21.6
(77.13 m.p.h.)	
L. Taveri (Kreidler)	29 24
(77.3 m.p.h.)	

Itoh's record race winning speed last year was 78.81 m.p.h., so the "targets" for today's riders are 79.10 m.p.h. for the lap and 78.81 for the three laps. Will anyone touch the "four-score"?

Non-starters, as shown in the list in column 5, have reduced the field to 20, but the "stars" are

Once again Shell-Mex and B.P. Ltd. chartered a helicopter to act as an air-ambulance during the races. The Westland Sikorsky S 55 Helicopter was based in the Depot Field alongside the Grandstand. Its use was controlled by the A.C.U. and landing grounds in the more inaccessible parts of the Course were mapped out.

If the air-ambulance was required, the A.C.U. Officials could call it into action by a direct radio telephone link and, with a doctor, two stretchers, first-aid equipment and blood plasma on board, the "Chopper" could be despatched within seconds.

Lew Ellis, the Shell-Mex and B.P. Racing Service Manager, said: "We provided this helicopter for the A.C.U. in the interest of the sport—and hoped that there would be no need for it to be used!"

Ballacraine, but Hugh Anderson (No. 3) is there only a second or so later, so he has obviously picked up quite a bit; and at Glen Helen he is announced as leading on the roads.

11.9 a.m.—now they've all reached Ballacraine. Stop watches on them at Kirk Michael.

No. 3, Hugh Anderson, is leading No. 2. Koshino by four seconds—i.e. 14 seconds on corrected time. No. 18, M. Itoh reaches Kirk Michael a minute and a half after Hugh, which means a corrected time loss of 20 seconds. It looks as if Hugh has a good lead.

The order at Sulby Bridge in Anderson (No. 3), Morishita (No. 7), Itoh (No. 18), Anscheidt and Koshino (Nos. 1 and 2; together) and Bryans (No. 5).

11.20 a.m.—ten riders have passed Ramsey, including No. 20, Provini, who had a rather slow start; he must be going well now, though.

At the Bungalow—about 11.2 a.m.—Anderson is obviously in

T.T. TERMS TRAVESTIED—By Jack Ketton

"A Fast 'Fifty'."

. . . .as recorded by Geoff Davison in that evening's edition of the "T.T. Special". . . .

ENTRIES IN THE 50 c.c. RACE

1. H. G. ANSCHEIDT Kreidler
2. H. KOSHINO .... Suzuki
3. H. R. ANDERSON ... Suzuki
4. A. PAGANI ... Mondal (N.S.)
5. R. BRYANS .... Honda
6. J. HUBERTS .... (N.S.)
7. I. MORISHITA .... Suzuki
8. D. A. SIMMONDS Tohatsu
9. L. TAVERI .... Kreidler
10. L. E. PLUMRIDGE .. Honda
11. L. JOHANSSON SNS (N.S.)
12. P. ESER ...... Honda (N.S.)
14. T. ROBB ...... Honda (N.S.)
15. C. C. W. MATES ...... Honda
16. N. TANIGUCHI .... Honda
17. M. J. SIMMONDS Tohatsu
18. M. ITOH .... Suzuki
19. D. A. JULER .... Itom
20. T. PROVINI ...... Kreidler
21. L. E. EVANS .... Honda
22. A. G. HUTCHINS ... Honda
23. A. DAWSON Sheene Sp (NS)
24. D. P. CLARKE Foster (N.S.)
25. J. PINK .... Honda
26. J. TOMPSETT .... Honda
27. P. HORSHAM .... Honda
28. P. J. FOSTER Foster (NS)
29. R. J. SMITH .... Honda

MOTOR CYCLE 18 JUNE 1964

MOTOR CYCLE 18 JUNE 1964

106   107

Records all the way

HUGH ANDERSON (Suzuki) has no intention of relinquishing his grip on that 50 cc world crown. He just blasted everyone else off the road when winning the 50 cc TT last Friday at 80.64 mph, with an astonishing record lap of 81.13 mph.

That's only a fraction of the story. Even more amazing was the feat of second man Ralph Bryans (Honda). In a last-lap spurt, he rocketed from sixth to second place, snatching it from Isao Morishita (Suzuki) by the incredibly close margin of 0.6s!

Although lacking in size, the fifties provided a closely fought road battle. Starting together, Harao Koshino (Suzuki) and Georg Anscheidt (Kreidler) had Anderson on their tails by Union Mills.

A few miles farther on, at Ballacraine, the hard-riding Kiwi had wedged himself between the leading pair then cheekily slipped ahead at Glen Helen. Anscheidt and Koshino slipstreamed the champ right through Kirkmichael and it was only on the Sulby straight that Anderson managed to get 200 yards ahead.

Already, the race had established a record—the field had swarmed through Ballacraine without a solitary retirement, the first time this had happened during the week! Considering that most of these engines were buzzing at anywhere between 12,000 and 19,000 rpm....

Overdrive

Down the Mountain. Anscheidt made full use of his overdrive top gear and shot past Koshino and Anderson.

Past the start, only 1s covered all three, although Anderson still had the advantage on corrected time. Anscheidt's effort was all the more praiseworthy, bearing in mind that he was using his spare engine, having damaged his best one in practice.

Rebuilt with new jewels and mainspring after the last practice session, Ralph Bryans' little twin was rapidly freeing up and he set about recovering the 10s starting advantage that he had lost to Morishita.

Through the start, Itoh and Taniguchi overtook Taveri who, like Anscheidt, had made his overdrive pay off down the Mountain.

Yes, it had to be a lap record. From a standing start,

Fastest in practice, last year's winner Mitsuo Itoh (Suzuki) finally managed to shake off Naomi Taniguchi (Honda), who had started with him, when they were over the Mountain. By Keppel Gate, Itoh had gobbled up the 40s starting interval between himself and Luigi Taveri (Kreidler).

Anderson chopped a fine 12.8s off Ernst Degner's (Suzuki) 1963 record, lapping in 28m 24.4s, 79.69 mph. The next three had all beaten the old record!

Only 8.4s behind Anderson came Itoh, with Anscheidt a mere 0.8s astern, then Koshino — wait for it — another 0.8s behind! Fifth, by 7.2s, Morishita had 6.8s in hand over Taniguchi, who had only 2.6s to spare over Bryans.

The leading trio on the road were still hard at it with Anscheidt and Koshino still challenging Anderson. Piling on the agony, Anderson inched ahead, gaining a 1s road advantage over Anscheidt.

The German gained a 10s advantage over Koshino, but closed the gap by the end of the lap was only 1s behind.

Anderson's advantage on corrected time was now a comfortable 36.4s, with Anscheidt second and Koshino third.

With his engine gradually losing its fine edge, Itoh had slipped to fourth, 5.4s astern of Kosh, and only 2.6s behind him came the diminutive Morishita with Bryans a further 3.6s back.

Buzzing

On this third visit to the TT, the Honda new boy was 12.6s astern of the second man, but his engine was now buzzing better than ever....

Marvellous; an over-81 mph lap! Anderson sliced 29.6s off that scorching opener —27m 54.8s, 81.10 mph. Now the average speeds of the first seven were all above the previous lap record!

Pulling trump cards from all angles, Bryans made meteoric progress to pick off the runners in front—on corrected time and on the road.

By Sulby the two were third and only 3s astern of Anscheidt. Only 2.6s behind was Morishita at the finish. He could pull back that 3s up the Mountain, but Anscheidt would have the edge down the other side. Bryans' task was eased by Anscheidt striking front-brake trouble in Ramsey —he dare not use it for fear of its sticking on. Itoh's engine was ailing, owing to a suspected stuck piston ring, and he slipped back to fifth behind Morishita.

Then the hard-riding Koshino fell at the fast 32nd Milestone but escaped with a severe shaking.

Morishita now speeded dramatically and went up to second place.

Would he, could he, do it? Down the Mountain, Bryans gained fractions on corrected time on Morishita. The crowd tensed. Anderson was already safely home, a popular winner. A rider appeared, flashed across the line—Bryans. Then. Long pause, watches checked—the narrowest of gnat's whiskers—0.6s.

Spare a thought for Georg Anscheidt. Only 2.6s behind Morishita at the finish, he found, on post-race examination, that his front brake was not so badly damaged, that he need not have been so cautious and the 3.2s separating him from second place could easily have been retrieved on braking alone.

A true disc jockey, Anderson belted out another record on that final lap, 27m 54.2s, 81.13 mph. And the average of the first six was comfortably inside the previous lap record.

A final record—out of 20 starters only two retired with mechanical trouble!

FINISHING ORDER

		h	m	s	mph
1	H. ANDERSON (Suzuki)	1	24	13.4	80.64
2	R. BRYANS (Honda)	1	25	14.8	79.68
3	I. MORISHITA (Suzuki)	1	25	8.8	79.67
4	H.G. Anscheidt (Kreidler)	1	25	23.4	79.63
5	M. Itoh (Suzuki)	1	25	32.4	79.57
6	N. Taniguchi (Honda)	1	26	33.0	77.39
7	L. Taveri (Kreidler)	1	26	39.6	74.92
8	T. Provini (Kreidler)	1	30	18.0	70.53
9	O.A. Simmonds (Tohatsu)	1	39	21.2	68.37
10	L.E. Plumridge (Honda)	1	39	30.4	68.31
11	P. Horsham (Honda)	1	39		65.00
12	J. Tompsett (Honda)	1	44	30.4	64.78
13	L.E. Evans (Honda)	1	44		62.88
14	A.G. Hutchings (Honda)	1	49	45.8	56.72
15	D.A. Juler (Itom)				

Fastest Lap.—Anderson, 27m 54.2s, 81.13 mph.
First-class Replicas.—Nos 1 to 8 inclusive (time limit: 1h 3m 45s).
Second-class Replicas.—Nos 9 to 11 inclusive (time limit: 1h 41m 0.4s).
Manufacturers' Team Prize.—Suzuki: Anderson, Morishita, Itoh. No club team finished intact.

In the later stages of the race, No 18, Mitsuo Itoh (Suzuki), and Naomi Taniguchi (Honda) were no farther apart than they are here, at Signpost Corner. Itoh finished fifth, Taniguchi sixth

Knee out, well out as usual, Hugh Anderson (Suzuki) attacks Bedstead Corner to win his second TT

Close scrap between No.5, Ralph Bryans (Honda), and No.7, Isao Morishita (Suzuki), here screaming through Cronk-ny-Mona. Bryans eventually took second spot from the Japanese by only 0.6s!

.... and next week's issue of "Motor Cycle" - "Records all the way"

Leaping Ballaugh Bridge, runner-up Ralph Bryans leads third man home, Isao Morishita.

Mitsuo Itoh challenged for another 50 cc victory, but was hampered by a suspect faulty piston ring and had to settle for fifth spot.

1965

The Suzuki effort for the 1965 TT was immense. Frank Perris recalled "We were entered in the usual three classes and each rider probably had two bikes per class. There were about seventeen bikes and there must have been about twenty mechanics plus the management team." Indeed, there were so many bikes that Suzuki had to take an extra garage at the Falcon Cliff Hotel to supplement the workshop at the Fernleigh hotel.

Thanks to Frank Perris, we now see a number of previously unpublished shots of the Suzuki stable. First of all, a line up of 50 cc, 125 cc and 250 cc machinery.

By 1965, the bikes occupied not only the Fernleigh's garage but also extra space at the nearby Falcon Cliff hotel. (Perris collection)

Three shots of the notorious "Whispering Death" from 1965. (Perris collection)

Perris on the start line of the 1965 Lightweight TT. Behind him stands the "King of Brands", Derek Minter, with his Cotton. Minter (winner of the race in 1962 on a Honda) finished ninth. (Perris collection)

Perris bump starts Whsipering Death, led away by his starting partner, Franta Stastny on the CZ, although it was entered as a Jawa. Despite losing fourth gear on lap one, Stastny came home in fifth place. (Perris collection)

Suzuki's team captain pulls out of the Gooseneck as he recovers from sixth place at the end of lap one (with an unscheduled pit stop to change plugs) to take third place. (Perris collection)

The team was now optimistic about its chances in the 250 class. Whispering Death, now dubbed RZ65, was equipped with eight speeds and was seemingly on the verge of attaining reliability, with Perris taking fourth in the US GP at Daytona, although he was lapped by the Yamaha duo of Read and Duff.

But it was not lacking in speed. Ahearn recalled "That 250 four cylinder, the best thing I ever rode, was flying. After days of sorting the thing out so it would do one lap without seizing and the eventually six laps, I was passing the Honda fours in a straight line. I thought 'This is a beaut; I'll give 'em a lap record'." He was timed at 139 mph through the MCN speed trap.

"For the race, everything was right. I planned to do one steady lap and then go for it to show what it could do but the plan went awry." The Friday evening practice session was held in teeming rain. "There was a slippery patch under the trees at Sarah's Cottage and I crashed on it." Jack was carted off to hospital suffering from concussion, thereby ruling himself out of the race.

On Monday afternoon's Lightweight TT, following Deubel's sidecar victory in the opening event of the series, lone wolf Perris, using Ahearn's engine, had an eventful opening lap. Caught out by his full seven gallon tank at Ballacraine, he wisely opted to take to the slip road, and then, from the Creg to the end of the lap, the two right hand plugs were playing up. But, having stopped in his pit to change them, he moved from sixth place on lap one to finish on the podium, behind Redman and Duff.

Two days later and Suzuki's hopes were high for the 125 cc event, with the RT65, the watercooled twin. Both Degner and Anderson had shattered the lap record in practice. But it was to be squad newcomer Yoshimi Katayama who posed the greatest threat to Read and Duff astride Yamaha's brand new untried twin cylinder models.

While Katayama ended the first lap in third place a whisker behind the Yamaha duo, team captain Perris did not reach Union Mills. Anderson's challenge effectively ended at the Guthrie memorial when he was obliged to change a plug; Degner, although in fifth place, was only twelve seconds down on leader Read.

The Suzuki threat stumbled on lap two when Katayama's rear tyre went flat at Creg-ny-Baa, causing him to tour in and retire. Meanwhile, Anderson was really motoring, with records on laps two and three lifting him to fifth place. Degner's luck was out, as he had to change a plug on the final lap and so he slipped to eighth place - the last of the works bikes. Read recorded Yamaha's maiden TT win.

Two days later and the 50 cc event, delayed by half an hour because of mist and rain, was a Honda-Suzuki battle. Suzuki paraded the RK65, a water-cooled twin cylinder job, 32.5 x 30 mm, 14 bhp revving at 16,500 rpm. Itoh was keen to repeat his 1963 success and had a 12 second lead over rival Taveri at the end of lap one. Alas, Itoh's twin lost its edge and he was obliged to splutter back to the pits to change plugs, while Taveri's hesitant Honda came on song, enabling the Swiss star to move into the lead.

Despite a comfortable lead, Taveri did not ease off, keen to take his third Tourist Trophy. Anderson bagged second spot, nearly a minute behind the Swiss ace, with Degner in third. The fourth Suzuki, Michio Ichino, was never in the picture and retired at Waterworks on the final lap. Fourth man home was Charlie Mates on an obsolete Honda single - more than 15 minutes behind Degner, illustrating the difference between the works bikes and the humble privateer steeds.

Hugh Anderson takes his RK65 to runner up spot in the 50 cc TT, 1965. . . .

. . . .while team-mate Itoh, having been an early leader, was obliged to retire.

In his final TT week in August 1966, Hugh Anderson recorded two third places. Here he is seen on the 125 cc twin, on which he finished behind the Yamaha pairing of Ivy and Read.

1966

The 1966 TT, delayed by the seamen's strike, so that it was sandwiched between the Ulster GP and the Manx GP at the end of August, was in many ways the beginning of the end for Suzuki Japan's GP efforts.

The team had withdrawn from the 250 cc fray in the middle of the 1965 season, thanks to, as Vic Willoughby described it, pulling no punches, "its abject failure to make a success of such an apparently invincible specification" - whereupon Yamaha developed its own watercooled square four quarter litre racer.

But the basically unchanged twin cylinder models were still competitive in the 50 cc (the RK66) and 125 cc (the RT66) classes.

Scribe Willoughby opined that on sheer riding ability the Suzuki challenge looked formidable but the trouble was that, in Bob McIntyre's immortal words, they had to wait for the bikes. "Motor Cycle" magazine's technical man reported that "their engineers are not alone in learning that it is one thing to copy the basic layout from MZs, the fount of modern two-stroke thinking, and even to refine it by investing much more money, but quite another to tame the two-stroke's temperament and make a substantial breakthrough."

In the Ultra-Lightweight race, the Yamaha squad opted to use the well-tried twins instead of the new, largely untested square four and their prudence was rewarded as Ivy, Read and Duff took first, second and fourth places.

Anderson was clearly competitive; in practice he managed only two trouble-free laps on the 125 (which was one more than he managed on the 50) but he did unofficially break the lap record. In taking the final place on the podium, he was only half a minute behind winner Ivy. Perris came home in fifth.

Two days later came the massed start 50 cc event. Bryans and Taveri were fast starters and only Anderson could stay with them, but his pistons nipped up at Rhencullen and Barregarrow and the engine lost its edge. He trailed the Honda teamsters into third. The other Suzuki squad members had mixed fortunes. Degner, suffering from too rich a mixture, had a plug foul on the Mountain on both laps two and three but managed to retain fourth spot. Katayama toured to retire at the pits at the end of lap two with a holed piston while new boy Anscheidt was obliged to pull out when his engine locked solid on the second descent of Bray Hill.

A brace of three year old ex-works Suzuki singles was entered by Suzuki GB for Tommy Robb and Chris Vincent. Alas, the sidecar star was laid low by ëflu and replaced by Barry Smith. Robb was in a safe fifth position until the final Mountain climb when he was obliged to change a plug, dropping him to eleventh. Robb recalled "After having helped develop the Honda twins, I found the Suzuki single to be hopelessly slow."

But the team was now on the verge of breaking up. Perris had given notice that he intended to retire at the end of the season and, when advised that bikes would not be made available for Monza, planned to turn out for Benelli, only to be held to his contract by Suzuki HQ.

Anderson, disenchanted by no fewer than fifteen IoM breakdowns in practice, and the loss of his ascendancy in the tiddler classes, decided to leave the GP arena. Degner, perhaps less inclined to take risks following his severe injuries, had not returned to his old form and agreed with his masters that it was time to hang up his leathers.

Fourth man home Ernst Degner in his final TT race, at Parliament Square. (Walter Radcliffe collection)

The 50 cc race, 1966: Quarter Bridge on lap one and Tommy Robb, on Suzuki GB's ex works single, leads the Suzuki Japan entered works twins of Anderson (3) , Degner (4) and Anscheidt (7). They had to surrender to the twin cylinder Honda four strokes of Bryans and Taveri.

Another Ramsey shot from the same race: Anscheidt and Katayama. (Walter Radcliffe collection)

Still at the seamen's strike TT, with Katayama astride the RK66 at Governor's Bridge. He was obliged to retire from the 50 cc race at the end of lap two with a holed piston.

1967 and team new boy Stuart Graham, astride the RT67, rides to second place in the Ultra-Lightweight event, a whisker behind Read.

1967

Suzuki's first problem for 1967 was that of how to replace its galaxy of imploding stars. By cutting back on its own race effort, bowing out of the 50 cc and 125 cc classes, Honda provided the answer. At the end of 1966, Stuart Graham initially found himself without a job but, on Anderson's recommendation, he was snapped up by Suzuki - to ride alongside Katayama and Anscheidt.

Suzuki's new vee-four cylinder 125 cc model was not ready for the Diamond Jubilee TT, and so, armed with the twin cylinder RT67, Graham and Katayama began Wednesday's Ultra-Lightweight race as distinct underdogs, with the Yamaha trio of Ivy, Read and newcomer Akiyasu Motohashi as hot favourites. Rumour had it that Ivy had been offered a £1,000 bonus if he established the first 100 mph lap on a 125.

But, by Ballaugh on lap one, it was dark horses Graham and Motohashi who shared the lead, with a sluggish start delaying Read, in third, with Ivy languishing in fourth. Katayama had shot his bolt by Sulby. The team's other entry, Mitsuo Itoh, had crashed his 50 in Thursday afternoon's practice session at Kerrowmoar when another machine, just ahead, seized. Itoh suffered a broken wrist and hence was a non-starter.

By the end of the lap, Ivy was out but, over the Mountain, Read had used the superior speed of the Yam. to offset the Suzuki's better handling and crossed the line to lead Graham by a second. Graham, perhaps irritated that nobody had tipped him to win, rode brilliantly between Ballacraine and Ballaugh to regain the lead, which he maintained to the end of lap two by a fifth of a second.

Through the Highlander on the final lap and Graham's engine suddenly cut onto one cylinder, delaying him and putting his race in jeopardy, but the offending plug soon cleared and he was off again, levelling with Read by Ramsey. There was nothing in it on that final lap and Graham crossed the line, having started forty seconds before his rival, hoping for his maiden TT victory. Alas for Suzuki, Read got to the chequered flag with three seconds to spare. Motohashi, in a splendid third place, was over two minutes behind the duellists.

Making amends for his disappointment two days earlier, Stuart Graham rides his RK67 to 50 cc victory. . . .

. . . . ahead of slightly disgruntled team-mate Hans-Georg Anscheidt.

One of the truly evocative TT photos - up there with Tenni on his 250 cc Guzzi howling down the Mountain or Bob McIntyre on the 500 cc Gilera at the bottom of Bray Hill. Anscheidt and Graham peel into Union Mills.

Until the closure of Murray's Museum in 2005, a marvellous large copy of that photo (autographed by both riders) adorned one wall. Here Peter Murray studies it and holds a photo of Stuart's famous father Les astride the 125 cc MV on which he won the TT in 1953.

Graham's only regret was that he believed that he could have ridden harder from Ramsey on the last lap had he realised how close he was to emulating his father's MV victory in the class in 1953.

But two days later came his sought-after victory. A Suzuki winner in the 50 cc event was almost a dead cert; the factory had entered reigning world champion Anscheidt, Katayama, Graham and the unfortunate Itoh on the RK67 models (an update of the 1966 works bike). Suzuki GB had entered Chris Vincent on one of the new production aircooled singles but he had, as last year, been replaced, this time by Tommy Robb. With Honda out of the class, it was left to the privateers to offer a challenge.

Team orders were that Katayama should be allowed to win the race, which began with a mass start. Despite numerous practice starts in the paddock, Katayama got away sluggishly in mid-pack, and Anscheidt and Graham were clear by Bray Hill.

They swept through Union Mills and were captured by the "Motor Cycle's" photographer tipping into the village, in one of the most evocative of all TT photos - see the edition of 22 June; for many years, a large print could be found in Murray's Museum by the Bungalow.

Meanwhile, having stopped to change a plug, Katayama, some two minutes behind his team-mates, set off in hot pursuit, with Robb in fourth ahead of the privateers who were predominantly riding production Hondas - the days of the Itoms and specials had already been consigned to history.

The two leaders were clearly waiting for their colleague - indeed Anscheidt ostentatiously sat up as he passed the Glencrutchery Road grandstand to complete the first lap.

After Ballacraine on lap two, Anscheidt's engine cut out onto one cylinder but it chimed in again when he landed heavily after Ballaugh Bridge! Katayama duly caught his mates between Ballaugh and Ramsey and confidently anticipated the win which team tactics had dictated.

But, on the Mountain Mile, turning to glance at Anscheidt's machine which was evidently ailing, Katayama drifted off the road into a ditch. As the startled Anscheidt and Graham slowed, "Yosh" climbed out of the ditch, gave them the thumbs up and off they went.

With his engine still cutting out and oil from the pump leaking onto the rear wheel, Anscheidt was slowing and Graham, tired of waiting, cleared off on lap three to record his cherished TT victory, with Anscheidt a minute behind and the third man on to the podium, Tommy Robb, a staggering fifteen minutes behind him.

Graham explained "Georg was, I think, a bit annoyed that I hadn't waited for him, but I was still irritated by losing Wednesday's race and I wasn't going to hang around."

So it was that Suzuki Japan's final race in the TT was crowned with success. At the end of the 1967 season, Suzuki, together with Honda Japan, pulled out of the GP arena.

The 50 cc prize-giving ceremony: Anscheidt, Graham and Robb - all looking slightly ill-at-ease, to tell the truth! (FoTTofinders)

EPILOGUE

Although the full Japanese works squad has never returned to Man Island, a couple of its bikes saw Manx action again, albeit with mixed results. In 1968, Suzuki gave Anscheidt both a 50 cc machine (on which he won the world championship) and a 125, while Graham was provided with a 125, to run on a private basis in International races. Suzuki lost interest in the machines and did not seek their return at season's end.

The Anscheidt bike, a 1966 RT66, was bought by Dieter Braun who used it to win the 1970 125 cc TT, en route to that year's world title. Braun's effort was exceptional, as he was a newcomer to the Mountain circuit.

Graham's bike was a 1967 RT67 but its post-works Mountain circuit career in the hands of another newcomer was markedly less auspicious than that of its stablemate. Graham sold it to the youthful Barry Sheene, who took it to the 1971 TT series, primarily seeking points for that season's title, for which he was a serious contender. As is well known, Sheene dropped the plot at Quarter Bridge on the second lap during a wet race and he vowed never to return.

Since Suzuki Japan's withdrawal, the marque has been represented in the TT by a succession of dealer/importer supported teams. Highlights have included the praiseworthy efforts of Eddie Crooks, sponsoring the likes of Frank Perris. Next, the Texaco Heron Suzuki squad achieved considerable success, primarily with the RG500, with star riders of the calibre of John Williams, Pat Hennen, Mike Hailwood, Graeme Crosby, Mick Grant and Rob McElnea. And, in more recent times when production based bikes have been to the fore, the TAS squad of Hector Neill and his son Philip has flown the Suzuki flag, with David Jefferies, Adrian Archibald, Bruce Anstey and Cameron Donald registering victories.

Suzuki as a marque has stayed loyal to the TT; 1990 saw its thirtieth anniversary at the TT which was marked by a celebration lap, while an exhibition in the "Suzuki Village", next to the main grandstand, was a feature of the 2000 TT. And, in 2007, Suzuki Sunday at the Castletown Golflinks Hotel featured (as well as the jazz band and welcome sustenance) a host of RG 500s, an ex-Graeme Crosby Formula One bike, a 1967 50 cc RK67 and the sole surviving completely original vee four 125 cc RS67 of 1967 vintage - together with a goodly number of the marque's star TT riders: Itoh, Perris, Stan Woods, Crosby, Anstey and Archibald, plus Kevin Schwantz, John Reynolds and Chris Walker.

Marvellous stuff; thanks, Suzuki. Here's to the next fifty years.

1970: a privateer victory for Dieter Braun, astride the ex-Anscheidt 125.

1971: Barry Sheene, astride the ex-Graham 125, en route to a spill at Quarter Bridge, which witnessed the conclusion of his brief association with the TT. (Racing Photos IOM)

A LESSON IN TT CIRCUITRY   June 1990

IN February 1960, a group of Japanese led by James Akira ('Jimmy') Matsumiya, the man given the job of putting Suzuki motorcycles on the European map, took the Steam Packet to the Island.

Their mission? To reconnoitre the entire TT course and to pick up whatever tips they could from Island experts like Geoff Duke.

Many Island residents still recall the Morris Minor 1000 hired by Matsumiya; at barely walking pace, it crawled around the Mountain course in freezing temperatures whilst a small Japanese gentleman sat cross-legged on the bonnet working a cine camera.

Shell, a committed Suzuki sponsor even then, sent their competitions manager to aid the party. It was Lew Ellis, a man who was always on or around the TT start line during TT fortnight right up to his death a few years ago.

During the visit, Ellis introduced the Suzuki party to the Fernleigh Hotel in Douglas where the Suzuki team stayed and had their workshops throughout the sixties.

After filming the course, having a lesson TT riding by the master Geoff Duke, the party familiarised themselves with Manx beer before leaving the Island. En-route to Heathrow, the party called on Lewis Leathers where Matsumiya equipped the Japanese riders with the latest style of racing leathers – all black of course.

> The 1990 Isle of Man TT is Suzuki's 30th year on the island, SIZZLING SIXTIES celebrates this anniversary with some interesting facts and figures from the first decade.

Matsumoto, Itoh and Ichino wearing their new leathers alongside the Suzuki Colleda just before leaving Japan for their 1960 Isle of Man TT race debut (Credit: Suzuki Motor Co.)

ISLAND DEBUT

IT was a racer based upon the Suzuki 125cc machine that was to introduce Suzuki to the racing world outside of Japan. An inexperienced three man team was to ride the machine which Suzuki had mistakenly entered as a Colleda – the roadster's model name – instead of Suzuki. Mitsuo Itoh (now in total control of Suzuki's racing activities), Michio Ichino and Toshio Matsumoto made Suzuki's Island debut but a practice spill side-lined Itoh and on Ellis' recommendation, a little-known scouse rider, Ray Fay was seconded to the fledgling team.

The 125cc TT was dominated by the works MV 4-strokes who trounced the two-stroke Colledas into 15th, 16th and 18th places.

Resolutely, Jimmy Matsumiya and his team returned to Japan determined to improve their machines and to gain experience before the 1961 TT races.

Publicity material for the thirtieth anniversary celebrations in 1990. . . .

.... the fortieth anniversary bash in 2000....

.... and the Centenary TT's Suzuki Sunday in 2007.

Seen in Castletown at Suzuki Sunday was the fantastic four cylinder vee-four 125, the RS67/68. . . .

. . . . and Mitsuo Itoh was an ever-obliging star of the show.

The wonderful Centenary TT concluded with the Parade of Champions which Itoh graced aboard a newly restored 50 cc RK67.

BIBLIOGRAPHY

For fans of Suzuki and the TT, there are two books which are "must haves":

Team Suzuki by Ray Battersby, 1982, ISBN 0-85045-416-6:
Re-published in 2008 by Parker House Publishing Inc, with ISBN 13: 978-0-9796891-5-4 and ISBN 10: 0-9796891-5-5.
This is not simply a "bike book"; it is a masterpiece It is the well-illustrated definitive history of the Suzuki works racers to 1981 (- technicalities, riders and races all comprehensively covered -) and is arguably the best single marque race history in the English language. See the website www.teamsuzuki.co.uk

TT100 by Mick Duckworth, 2007, ISBN 1-899602-67-4:
By a very considerable distance, the best of the numerous TT histories which appeared in 2007 to mark the event's centenary. It does not pretend to be a chronicle of each of the races; instead it is a profusely (and cleverly) illustrated celebration of the world's greatest road races, packed with anecdotes, personalities and asides, capturing the atmosphere and spirit of the unique event. Unparalleled as a TT review; a work of art.

We are sometimes asked to recommend exceptional motorcycle race histories. In recent years, many books covering racing motorcycles and their riders have been published; sadly, too many are superficial, ill-researched and badly written - e.g. how many times must we read of "MV Augusta"? Fortunately, there is also a fair number of excellent publications and, in addition to the couple mentioned above, no serious enthusiast should be without the following top ten (all of which are large format and lavishly illustrated):

1. American Racer 1900 to 1939 by Stephen Wright, 1989, ISBN 0-87938-376-3
Detailed captions complement wonderful photos of the American board racers, Jake de Rosier etc.

2. Le Moto da Corsa al Circuito del Lario 1921-1939 by Sandro Colombo, 1991.
Italian language; not simply a history of the Circuit of Lario (the Italian TT) but also a review of the eminent racing motorcycles of the two decades during which it was run.

3. Gilera Quattro by Sandro Colombo, 1992, ISBN 88-86184-00-X
Italian language. Wonderful history of the four cylinder Gilera, one of racing's foremost machines, from the OPRA of the 1920s, via the CNA Rondine, to Remor's post War version, the domination of Masetti, Duke and McIntyre to the under-financed efforts of the 1960s. Written by the Arcore team's chief engineer of the early 1950s.

4. Moto Guzzi da corsa: tutti i modelli dal 1921 al 1940, by Sandro Colombo, 1995, ISBN 88-7911-134-5
Italian language. Covers what it says on the tin: pre-War Guzzi race bikes, Woods, Tenni and the rest.

5. Dorino Serafini by Franco Andreatini, 1997.
Italian language. The biography of Gilera's European champion of 1939 within the context of racing in Italy in the 1930s; also covers his post-War Ferrari career.

6. Moto Guzzi da corsa: tutti i modelli dal 1941 al 1957, by Sandro Colombo, 1998, ISBN 88-7911-181-7
Italian language. Second part of Sandro Colombo's definitive Guzzi GP race history; the straight four, the vee eight, Lorenzetti, Lomas - all here.

7. 100 years of Czech Motorcycle Sport, 2004, ISBN 80-902516-8-4
Czech language, with limited English text. Wonderfully illustrated history of racing in Czechoslovakia - fabulous public roads circuits, 500 cc supercharged Jawa, Stastny, Havel etc.

8. Montjuic, 2004, ISBN 84-933224-4-X
Spanish language, with limited English text. Comprehensive history of racing at Montjuich Park: 24 hours, GPs, endurance etc

9. Colin Seeley: Racer. . . . and the rest, 2006, ISBN 0-9544357-1-0
Full of fascinating snippets of racing in the 1960s; naturally, sidecars well to the fore - e.g. wonderful tales of the exploits of Seeley's buddy, the eccentric Florian Camathias - and not the usual superficial coverage of the three wheeled art.

10. L'Epopee Moto: Les annees Jules Tacheny, 2008, ISBN 978-2-8741-5995-4
French language. Based on the career of Jules Tacheny, FN star of the 1930s and subsequently supremo of the prestigious Mettet road races; but also surveys the vibrant pre-War Belgian racing scene, which has been undeservedly ignored by the classic magazines.

ILKLEY RACING BOOKS SERIES: CORRECTIONS:

It has been brought to our attention that a number of errors occur in the Ilkley Racing series of books covering classic motorcycle racing. We apologise and now correct them as follows:

Benelli Road Racers: page 77: the machine which Tarquinio Provini used in practice for the 1965 Junior TT was probably not a 251 cc model but simply a Lightweight bike, entered in the 350 cc class primarily to give "Old Elbows" extra practice.

Vostok Road Racers: pages 7 and 8: it is stated (relying on information provided by the Riga Motor Museum) that the single cylinder of the S-154's engine of 1954 was inclined slightly forwards and that the subsequent 125 cc S-157 engine stood vertically. However, some factory drawings and photos (although not all) suggest that the S-154 engines were vertical and the S-157 versions were inclined.

It is also stated that the S-159 may have been designed and built with the help of the Jawa factory. In fact, it is more likely that the S-159 was a simple clone of the 125 cc CZ model 855. The engine featured the same bore and stroke dimensions and the same characteristic shaft drive to the exhaust cam on the right hand side.

Vostok Road Racers: page 20: Franta Stastny's ride in the Lightweight TT in 1957 was of course over the Clypse circuit, not the Mountain.

The TT Races: page 14; the photo is not of Stanley Woods in the 1922 Junior TT. We regret that we have so far been unable to identify the rider.

1907 TT: in the interests of accuracy, we also wish to mention one commonly-made error relating to TT history. A number of books seek to illustrate "the beginning of it all" with a photograph which purports to show numbers one and two, Frank Hulbert and Jack Marshall respectively, on the start line at St Johns, seconds before the first TT got underway on 28 May, 1907 - see, for instance, Mac McDiarmid's "The Magic of the TT", Bill Snelling's "The TT in old photographs" and Stuart Barker's "TT Century". However, the photo is one of Charlie Collier and Rem Fowler (as the previous year's winners) starting the 1908 race - see the almost identical shot published in "The Motor Cycle" of 30 September 1908. Congratulations to Morton's "TT07 Island Racer" which featured, and correctly identified, a photo of the 1907 start.

OUR SPONSORS:

About S.C.S.: It is an Isle of Man registered company specialising in all aspects of the building services industry. It provides a comprehensive service dealing with plumbing and heating, and servicing, building and electrical work. S.C.S. has major contracts with the government, the finance sector and retail and manufacturing services. S.C.S. can be contacted at Ballannette Park, Baldrine. Ballannette is a wildlife habitat in natural wetlands which has been developed so as not to disturb the native and visiting birdlife. It is open to the public. Visit the wetlands park and the website at www.scs.co.im

About Ilkley Racing: It is a team of road racing enthusiasts which, over a period of twenty years, has entered a variety of interesting machinery in some of the classic pure road races. Sponsored riders have included Mick Noblett (8th in the 1994 Singles TT on a 558 cc Gilera Piuma), Patrick Sproston (250 cc Aermacchi, Mettet) and Michael Schofield (350 cc TZ Yamaha, Chimay). It has also published a series of books covering the Golden Era of motorcycle racing. Copies can be obtained from the publisher.

About Mannin Collections Racing: Run by Mike Kelly and Alan Kelly, Mannin Collections, which is based in Peel, offers Manx memorabilia, including TT related items. For many years, Mannin Collections Racing has been a keen supporter of the TT, sponsoring leading riders such as Ian Lougher and Chris Palmer, with a number of victories in the Lightweight classes to its credit.